The
Complete Book
of
Spices:

Their Medical,
Nutritional
and Culinary Uses

Other Keats Books of Relevant Interest

The
Complete Book
of
Spices:

Their Medical,
Nutritional
and Culinary Uses

JOHN HEINERMAN
Introduction by Henry Heimlich, M.D.

Keats Publishing, Inc. New Canaan, Connecticut

The information in this book is not intended as medical advice. Its intention is solely informational and educational. It is assumed that the reader will consult a medical or health professional should the need for one be warranted.

Library of Congress Cataloging in Publication Data
Heinerman, John.
    The complete book of spices.

    Bibliography: p. 163
    Includes index.
    1. Herbs—Therapeutic use.   2. Cookery (Herbs)
    3. Spices.   I. Title.

RM666.H33H44   1983   615'.321   82-80700
ISBN 0-87983-281-9

**The Complete Book of Spices: Their
Medical, Nutritional and Culinary Uses**

Printed in the United States of America

Keats Publishing, Inc., 27 Pine Street (Box 876)
New Canaan, Connecticut 06840

Dedicated To
The Lamanite Boy

Spices illustrated on the cover

1. Sage	**2.** Nutmeg	**3.** Bay leaves	**4.** Cayenne	**5.** Thyme
6. Cinnamon	**7.** Cardamom	**8.** Star Anise	**9.** Garlic	**10.** Juniper

Contents

Publisher's Note

Simple herbal remedies are frequently used in the initial stages of disease, when a person is not in a stage of serious ill-health, nor in need of immediate emergency medical treatment.

The intended use of this book among general readers does not include self-treatment of complicated diseases. The mention of herbal treatments is for educational interest, and to suggest the methods of treatment employed in those societies in which herbal treatment is the sole means of medical knowledge.

It cannot be stressed enough, however, that in the case of serious illness, a physician or other practitioner of your choice should be consulted.

Foreword

Spices and herbs have been part of the medical armamentarium of almost every civilization. In many countries these natural medications have been in continuous use. In developing countries where Western medicine has not gained acceptance owing to tradition and prohibitive cost, the use of natural remedies has remained predominant in patient care. The potency of some herbal medications is illustrated by digitalis and quinine which have proved effective in the treatment of such serious and widespread conditions as heart disease and malaria.

In the United States and other Western countries there is a resurgence of interest in natural medicines; this is one of the changes brought about by the holistic health movement. The use of natural medicines also represents a rebellion against the deleterious side effects and complications resulting from some of the chemical "wonder drugs," as well as their cost. This trend is further evidenced by the revived interest in homeopathic medicine that has been stimulated by the book *Homeopathic Medicine at Home* (J.P. Tarcher, Inc.) by Maesimund B. Panos, M.D. and Jayne Heimlich.

John Heinerman has accumulated and described information concerning scores of spices and herbs. His in-depth research is evidenced by his carefully prepared bibliography. Mr. Heinerman was not satisfied to simply review the work of others, but has travelled throughout the world in order to present the results of firsthand knowledge and investigation.

Not being an authority in the field I cannot render an opinion regarding the effectiveness, actions or contents of the herbs and spices described, nor can I comment on Mr. Heinerman's personal observations. It can be said with certainty, however, that *The Complete Book of Spices* provides an extensive accumulation of information concerning the uses of herbs and spices, and will serve as a valuable reference for all interested in this subject for many years to come.

Henry Heimlich, M.D.
Professor of Advanced Clinical Sciences,
Xavier University, Cincinnati, Ohio

Introduction

To my knowledge no one has yet compiled an alphabetical reference guide to the use of herbs and spices in the treatment of major and minor health problems. History amply demonstrates that many herbal substances ordinarily used primarily as spices in food preparation, have significant clinical value as well. Often herbs serve a dual purpose as a food and a medicine.

The ancients never did distinguish between the herbs used for their food, and those employed in healing of the sick. To them, what you ate also made you well. The noted Harvard pathologist Dr. Guido Majno has pointed out that the Greeks used one lovely word, *aromata*, to cover *all* of what we would call perfume, spices, herbs, drugs and incense.

In this book, I have presented information on approximately fifty-nine herbs, giving both their medicinal and culinary applications; a third section is added to provide the chemical and nutritional data for these herbs.

In collecting this information, I have used both medical and folk sources, taken from existing books, as well as my own firsthand experience in the field. I have especially drawn on my recent trips to the Soviet Union, the People's Republic of China, Ethiopia and Mexico. Correspondent colleagues in Pakistan and India have also shared their information for inclusion in this book.

A recent Public Broadcasting Corporation special titled "The Doctors of Nigeria" revealed a fascinating amount of information on how the traditional healers of that country apply herbs for an astonishing array of ailments—from yellow fever to broken bones, even cancer.

This television report, which was part of the *Nova* series, showed the Nigerian healers at work on their patients and attending a medical conference at Lagos. The impression one received was that these native practitioners are just as capable of treating major illnesses with their herbs, as are the licensed medical doctors with university training who use prescription drugs. As a medical anthropologist, I share these sentiments; in my sojourns to the hot, steamy jungles of Mexico and Ethiopia, or speaking with noted Russian scientists in their plant-filled laboratories, and in the land of the Great Wall and the Forbidden City—all of my experiences only confirm and reinforce what I have believed for a long time: the primitive can be just as effective as the sophisticated.

By some estimations, modern medical science has become far too complicated for even the most knowledgeable people to grasp and understand. In fact, the student journal of the American Medical Association, *The New Physician*, had this to say about the enormous complexities facing modern doctors, in the November 1980 issue: "An information explosion in the last twenty years is putting tremendous 'time pressure' on students, and neither physicians nor students know how to cope with the overwhelming amount of new information they are being required to learn."

Fortunately for us, herbal medicine is not that complicated. It is quite impressive to note that the uses of cinnamon, namely, for diarrhea, nausea and bleeding of the womb, have never really changed in some 4,000 years. A review of recorded history will reveal that these uses for cinnamon were the *same* in the days of the Assyrians (1,000 B.C.), the Egyptians (300 B.C.), the Romans (time of Christ), and the Arabs (A.D. 1,100), as they are now at the end of the twentieth century.

Thus it is safe to say that the information contained in this book is unlikely to change in terms of the therapeutic applications suggested. Yes, it may be that some new uses for cinnamon may be discovered a few years, or a few centuries into the future. And some new compounds may yet be isolated from this spice by curious scientists around the world. But all of such new information put together with what we already know cannot complicate herbal medicine to the degree that modern medicine has been inundated with tons of new knowledge.

While the pursuit of new knowledge cannot be denied as a relatively good thing, yet in all seriousness it must be asked to what depth we should probe in our endless quest for more facts. The prophets of old spoke about the knowledge of the wise being turned backward into foolishness (Isaiah 44:25). The present efforts of scientific research seem similarly futile—"Ever learning, and never able to come to the knowledge of the Truth" (Timothy 3:7).

There are three major sections to *The Complete Book of Spices*. The first section deals with the medical application of herbal spices. One may consult from an extensive alphabetical listing of disease conditions, next to which are given the spices which may be used to treat these same conditions. Once you have selected the herb, or herbs, you wish to use, then turn to the particular herb in the first section, which will give you specific directions for preparing and applying the herb.

The second section gives many of the culinary, or food, uses of each of the spices, which are listed, followed by the suggestions for implementing them in your food dishes.

The third section, combines all of the biochemical and nutritional data that is available for each of the spices. If you desire to know what the vitamin content of a spice is, its mineral content and similar data, you may look these up in the third section.

The information given with each entry does not necessarily guarantee a cure, nor medically-recommended treatment for the health problems mentioned. However, it does suggest a possible solution which, under most circumstances, is quite safe and certainly inexpensive. Please keep in mind, however, that these spices will not always elicit the same type of response from everyone, since individual metabolisms behave differently. So what may work for one person may not work for another.

Recently while awaiting a connecting flight in London, I read in the international issue of *Time* magazine that the American Medical Association had decided to drop their old injunction against members associating professionally with anyone who does not practice a "method of healing founded on scientific basis." But it was the sentence that followed which stirred my heart and brought out the urge to champion traditional folk methods of healing wherever I could. Commenting on the new change adopted by the A.M.A., *Time* magazine stated: "That leaves physicians free to refer patients to, as well as receive patients from, chiropractors, acupuncturists, *herbalists*, even faith healers" (Emphasis mine).

This incident reminds me of a statement by the famous Archbishop of Brazil, Dom Helder Camara: "Truth is alive and suffering. It is as important to free the truth from systems of thought which suffocate it, as it is to free men from inhuman imprisonment to the death."

By dropping that injunction, the A.M.A. has released its member physicians from the stranglehold of prejudice, and given them the freedom to pursue aspects of folk medicine as much as they may desire to do so. This form of sweet liberty was echoed nearly 2,000 years ago by the greatest champion of liberty who ever lived: "Know the truth and the truth shall make you free."

John Heinerman
Salt Lake City, Utah

The Complete Book of Spices:

Their Medical, Nutritional and Culinary Uses

Be thou like a roe or a young hart
upon the mountains of spices.
        —The Song of Solomon 8:14
        (*King James Bible*)

SECTION ONE

Medical Applications

This first section is in two parts. The first part consists of an alphabetical list of various health problems, with the herbs and spices used to treat them listed alongside the disease name. Look under this list until you find the disease, and then, after reading which herbs are used to treat it, you may turn to the second part, for specific directions on how to prepare the remedy.

The second part is an alphabetical listing of each of the herbs and spices, giving the common name, botanical name, part used, predominant characteristics, and the methods used in application for various ailments.

To learn how to make the various preparations, such as infusion, decoction and so forth, as well as how to collect and prepare culinary herbs and spices, refer to the Appendix at the end of the book.

PART ONE

Applications of Herbs and Spices in Diseases

Abdominal cramps: Dill, fennel, Ginger, Juniper, Pickling Spice, Spearmint.

Abortion (to prevent): Chives.

Abscess: See wounds; sores.

Acne: See blood purifiers; rash.

Adjuvant for other herbs: Cardamom, Coriander, Fennel.

Alcoholism: Angelica, Chinese Angelica, Thyme (*see also* blood purifiers; cirrhosis of the liver; nervous disorders).

Allergies: Burdock, Slippery Elm (*see also* hay fever; poison ivy/ oak/ sumac).

Anemia: Angelica, Chives, Dandelion, Fenugreek, Kelp, Watercress.

Antibacterial agent: Sage.

Antibiotic-herbal immunization: Garlic, Kelp.

Antidote for strong herbs: Coriander.

Antiseptic: Juniper, Onion, White Mustard.

Antiseptic: Basil, Juniper.

Aperients (to assist): Allspice, Coriander, Black Pepper, Pumpkin Pie Spice.

Appendicitis: Fenugreek, Slippery Elm.

Appetite (to improve): Allspice, Angelica, Anise, Black Pepper, Capsicum, Caraway, Cardamom, Celery seed, Chives, Coriander, Dandelion, Dill, Fennel, Garlic, Horseradish, Juniper, Marjoram, Rosemary, Saffron, Savory, Tarragon, Watercress, White Mustard (*see also* indigestion; intestinal gas; heartburn).

Arthritis: Angelica, Black Pepper, Burdock, Capsicum, Chinese Angelica, Coriander, Cumin, Fennel, Horseradish, Juniper, Peppermint, Sunflower, Sweet Marjoram, Thyme, Turmeric (*see also* neuralgia; rheumatism; sciatica).

1

Asthma: Angelica, Anise, Caraway, Dandelion, Garlic, Ginger, Horseradish, Lovage, Marjoram, Rosemary, Savory, Sunflower, Watercress (*see also* bronchitis; lung congestion).

Atherosclerosis: Capsicum, Garlic, Nutmeg, Onion, Watercress (*see also* heart attack; heart stimulant; cholesterol; blood purifiers).

Athlete's foot: See fungus; skin; rash.

Backache: Black Mustard, Capsicum, White Mustard (*see also* rheumatism; sciatica).

Bad breath: Allspice, Angelica, Anise, Caraway, Cardamom, Dill, Fennel, Mace, Pumpkin Pie Spice, Rosemary, Tarragon.

Bad dreams: Anise.

Bedwetting: Fennel.

Black-and-blue marks: See skin discolorations; bruises; wounds.

Bleeding: Angelica, Chives, Cinnamon, Kelp, Pumpkin Pie Spice, Saffron, Sage, Slippery Elm.

Blood circulation (to stimulate): Capsicum, Ginger, Mace, Nutmeg, Pickling Spice, Rosemary.

Blood clotting (to cause): Fenugreek, Kelp, Slippery Elm.

Blood clotting (to prevent): Capsicum, Ginger.

Blood purifiers: Borage, Burdock, Crab Apple, Dandelion, Lovage, Thyme, Turmeric, Watercress.

Boils: Burdock, Lovage.

Breast milk (to diminish flow): Parsley.

Breast milk (to increase flow): Anise, Basil, Borage, Caraway, Dill, Fennel.

Breathing difficulties: Black Mustard, Caraway, Fennel, Garlic, Onion.

Bronchitis: Angelica, Anise, Caraway, Chinese Angelica, Cinnamon, Cloves, Ginger, Lovage, Marjoram, Onion, Rosemary, Saffron, Sage, Savory, Slippery Elm, Thyme, White Mustard (*see also* asthma; lung congestion).

Bruises: Bay, Celery seed, Cinnamon, Fenugreek, Lemon Balm.

Bubonic plague: See epidemics.

Bunions: See corns.

Burns: Burdock, Onion, Pumpkin Pie Spice, Slippery Elm, Sunflower, Thyme (*see also* infection; rash).

Bursitis: See arthritis; neuralgia; rheumatism; sciatica.

Calluses: See corns.

Cancer: Angelica, Capsicum, Crab Apple, Garlic, Lovage, Parsley, Slippery Elm, Sunflower, Watercress (*see also* infection; rash).

Canker sores: See mouth sores.

Capsicum substitute: Ginger.

Carbuncles: Burdock.

Cavities: See toothache (and tooth decay).

Chemotherapy (against side effects of): Anise, Caraway, Chinese Angelica, Turmeric (*see also* nausea).

Chest (heart pains): Ginger.

Chickenpox: Burdock, Capsicum, Garlic, Ginger, Kelp, Oregano, Spearmint (*see also* measles; mumps).

Childbirth (to ease): Basil, Burdock, Chinese Angelica (*see also* breast milk; pregnancy).

Chill (coldness): See hypothermia.

Cholesterol: Chives, Coriander, Crab Apple, Fenugreek, Garlic, Marjoram, Onion, Sunflower, Turmeric (*see also* obesity).

Circulation: See blood circulation; atherosclerosis; hypothermia.

Cirrhosis of the liver: Chinese Angelica, Dandelion, Parsley, Sunflower, Thyme.

Cod-liver oil substitute: Fenugreek.

Colic: See intestinal gas.

Colitis: Capsicum, Fenugreek, Ginger, Slippery Elm (*see also* inflammation).

Coma: Bay, Black Pepper.

Common cold: Capsicum, Chili Powder, Garlic, Ginger, Juniper, Paprika, Pickling Spice, Sage, Savory, Sesame, Sunflower, Thyme, Turmeric (*see also* influenza).

Conjunctivitis: See eye infection.

Constipation: Anise, Basil, Chinese Angelica, Dandelion, Pickling Spice, Slippery Elm, White Mustard, White Pepper.

Convulsions: See epilepsy; hysteria; nervous disorders; spasms.

Corns: Dandelion, Garlic.

Cough: Anise, Borage, Cinnamon, Fennel, Ginger, Horseradish, Juniper, Lovage, Onion, Parsley, Rosemary, Slippery Elm, Thyme, Turmeric (*see also* whooping cough).

Cramps: Angelica, Anise, Bay, Capsicum, Coriander, Dill, Fennel, Ginger, Oregano, Pickling Spice, Rosemary, Sage, Spearmint (*see also* childbirth; indigestion; spasms).

Cuts: see wounds.

Cystitis: Lovage.

Cysts: See blood purifiers; rash.

Dandruff: Bay, Juniper, Parsley, Rosemary (*see also* hair-scalp problems; rash; ringworm).

Deafness: Angelica, Bay.

Debility: See weakness.

Diabetes: Allspice, Coriander, Dandelion, Fenugreek, Garlic, Juniper, Onion, Pumpkin Pie Spice, Thyme.

Diarrhea: Caraway, Cinnamon, Cloves, Coriander, Garlic, Ginger, Kelp, Mace, Nutmeg, Sage, Savory, Slippery Elm, White Oak Bark.

Digestion: Allspice.

Dizziness: Anise, Black Pepper, Lemon Balm, Peppermint, Sage.

Dreams: See insomnia.

Dropsy: See edema.

Drug addiction: Burdock (blood cleanser), Chaparral, Goldenseal (unless hypoglycemic), Lemon Balm, Oregano (antidote for drugs), Peppermint (to calm), Slippery Elm (nutrient) (*see also* blood purifiers; nausea; nervous disorders; hysteria).

Ear (inflammation of): Basil.

Earache: Basil, Bay, Cloves, Garlic, Spearmint (*see also* deafness).

Eczema: See rash.

Edema: Allspice, Anise, Burdock, Dandelion, Garlic, Horseradish, Juniper.

Electric Shock: Angelica, Curry Powder, Garlic, Peppermint, Turmeric (*see also* epilepsy; heart attack; hysteria; paralysis; shock; venomous bites).

Emaciation: Capsicum, Kelp, Slippery Elm.

Emotional disturbances: See mental-emotional disorders.

Emphysema: Angelica, Capsicum, Garlic, Lemon Balm, Thyme (*see also* asthma; bronchitis; lung congestion).

Epidemics: Angelica, Garlic, Juniper, Thyme.

Epilepsy: Angelica, Anise, Bay, Curry Powder, Garlic, Juniper, Oregano, Peppermint, Sage (*see also* spasms).

Esophagus (cancer of): Chinese Angelica.

External swellings: Parsley

Eye infection: Burdock, Fennel, Lovage, Parsley, Turmeric.

Eye inflammation: Borage, Fennel, Lovage, Slippery Elm.

Eyesight (to improve): Angelica, Borage, Parsley, Savory, Sesame, Slippery Elm (*see also* night blindness).

Fainting spells: Cinnamon, Garlic, Lemon Balm, Lovage, Peppermint (*see also* epilepsy).

Female problems: Bay, Caraway, Chinese Angelica, Cinnamon, Garlic, Marjoram, Saffron, Thyme (*see also* childbirth; leucorrhea; menstruation).

Fevers: Angelica, Black Pepper, Borage, Chili Powder, Chinese Angelica, Fenugreek, Garlic, Juniper, Kelp, Lovage, Mace, Nutmeg, Peppermint, Saffron, Sage, Savory, Slippery Elm, Spearmint, Sunflower, Thyme, White Pepper.

Flatulence: See intestinal gas.

Flavoring for bitter herbs: Caraway, Cardamom, Tarragon.

Fleas: See lice.

Flu: See influenza.

Fluid retention: See edema.

Food poisoning: Fennel (*see also* venomous bites).

Forgetfulness: See memory.

Frigidity: See sexual desire (diminished).

Frostbite: Allspice, Chili Powder.

Fungus (skin): Angelica, Cinnamon, Dandelion.

Fungus (toenails, fingernails): Bay.

Gallbladder (to stimulate): Fennel, Garlic, Lemon Balm, Onion, Peppermint, Pickling Spice, Sunflower.

Gallstones (to dissolve): Dandelion, Fennel, Lovage, Parsley.

Gangrene: Fennel, Garlic, Kelp, Slippery Elm, Thyme.

Gas: See intestinal gas.

Gastroenteritis: Angelica, Basil, Borage, Garlic, Kelp, Marjoram, Peppermint, Sage, Savory (*see also* indigestion; inflammation; heartburn).

Gonorrhea: See venereal disease.

Gout: Allspice, Angelica, Burdock, Celery seed, Coriander, Fennel, Fenugreek, Horseradish, Marjoram, Parsley, Saffron, Thyme, Turmeric, Watercress.

Gums (disease of): See infection; oral hygiene.

Hair loss: Burdock, Rosemary, Sage.

Hair-scalp problems (oily, itchy): Juniper, Parsley, Rosemary (*see also* dandruff).

Halitosis: See bad breath.

Hardening of the arteries: See atherosclerosis.

Hay fever: Kelp (*see also* allergies).

Headaches: Basil, Black Pepper, Cardamom, Chinese Angelica, Dill, Fennel, Ginger, Lemon Balm, Oregano, Peppermint, Rosemary, Sage, Savory, Watercress.

Heart attack: Chili Powder, Curry Powder, Garlic, Ginger, Peppermint.

Heart stimulants: Angelica, Borage, Capsicum, Coriander, Garlic, Juniper, Peppermint, Rosemary, Saffron (*see also* atherosclerosis; heart attack).

Heartburn: Angelica, Cardamom, Lovage, Peppermint (*see also* intestinal gas).

Heat (excess of): See fevers.

Heat loss: See hypothermia.

Heavy metal poisoning: See poisoning.

Hemorrhage: See bleeding.

Hemorrhoids: Burdock, Onion, Spearmint.

Hepatitis: See jaundice-hepatitis.

Hiccoughs: Anise, Garlic, Spearmint.

High blood pressure: See hypertension.

Hives: Angelica, Celery seed, Fenugreek, Juniper, Onion, Peppermint, Slippery Elm, Watercress (*see also* blood purifiers; rash).

Hoarseness: Fennel, Fenugreek, Garlic, Ginger, Horseradish, Juniper, Onion, Sage, Savory, Thyme.

Hot flashes: See female problems.

Hydrophobia: See rabies.

Hyperacidity: See heartburn; indigestion.

Hyperactivity: See nervous disorders.

Hypertension: Bay, Garlic, Onion, Parsley.

Hyperthermia: See fevers.

Hypoglycemia: Angelica, Ginger, Pumpkin Pie Spice.
Hypothermia: Allspice, Chili Powder, Mace, Nutmeg,
  Peppermint, Pickling Spice.
Hysteria: Angelica, Bay, Burdock, Celery seed, Lemon
  Balm, Oregano, Peppermint, Thyme (*see also* nervous
  disorders).

Impotency: See sexual desire (deficient).
Indigestion: Angelica, Basil, Bay, Black Mustard, Black Pepper,
  Capsicum, Cardamom, Cinnamon, Dandelion, Dill,
  Fennel, Ginger, Horseradish, Juniper, Kelp, Lovage,
  Marjoram, Oregano, Parsley, Peppermint, Pumpkin
  Pie Spice, Rosemary, Saffron, Sage, Savory,
  Spearmint, Turmeric, White Mustard. (*see also*
  appetite—poor; heartburn; intestinal gas).
Infant colic: Dill, Marjoram, Paprika, Spearmint.
Infection: Annatto, Basil, Cumin, Fennel, Garlic, Ginger,
  Horseradish, Kelp, Lemon Balm, Sesame, Thyme.
Infectious childhood diseases: Marjoram.
Inflammation: Borage, Coriander, Fenugreek, Garlic, Lovage,
  Slippery Elm, Spearmint, Sunflower, Turmeric (*see also*
  ulcers).
Influenza: Borage, Capsicum, Chili Powder, Fennel, Garlic,
  Ginger, Pickling Spice, Saffron, Sage, Savory, Sesame,
  Thyme.
Insanity: See hysteria; nervous disorders; mental-emotional
  problems; stress.
Insect bites and stings: See venomous bites.
Insect repellents: Anise, Bay, Black Pepper, Fennel, Garlic,
  Thyme.
Insomnia: Anise, Celery seed, Dandelion, Dill, Lemon Balm,
  Marjoram, Oregano, Peppermint, Pumpkin Pie Spice,
  Tarragon, Thyme.
Internal bleeding: Cinnamon.
Intestinal gas: Allspice, Anise, Cardamom, Cinnamon,
  Coriander, Cumin, Dill, Paprika, Peppermint,
  Pickling Spice, Rosemary, Saffron, Sage, Savory,
  Spearmint, Turmeric.
Intestinal mucus: Black Pepper, Capsicum, Chives, Lovage,
  Slippery Elm.
Intestinal pain: Chinese Angelica.

Intestinal purifiers: Angelica, Anise, Fennel, Garlic, Onion, Thyme.
Intestinal worms: See worms.
Itching: See rash; venomous bites.

Jaundice-hepatitis: Borage, Dandelion, Parsley, Sunflower (*see also* liver stimulant).

Kidney inflammation/infection: Paprika, Sunflower.
Kidney stones: Burdock, Celery seed, Dandelion, Garlic, Horseradish, Juniper, Parsley, Spearmint, Watercress (*see also* gallstones).

Lactation: See breast milk.
Laryngitis: See hoarseness.
Laxative: Anise.
Lead-mercury poisoning: Garlic, Kelp, Onion, Slippery Elm.
Leprosy: Burdock, Fennel, Garlic, Thyme.
Lesions: See scar tissue.
Leucorrhea: Fenugreek, Juniper, Lemon Balm, Sage, Slippery Elm.
Lice: Angelica, Anise, Bay, Black Pepper, Dill, Parsley, Sesame (*see also* insect repellent).
Liver diseases: See cirrhosis; jaundice-hepatitis.
Liver stimulants: Angelica, Anise, Annatto, Burdock, Dandelion, Fennel, Garlic, Horseradish, Juniper, Lemon Balm, Lovage, Onion, Peppermint, Pickling Spice, Rosemary, Slippery Elm, Turmeric.
Lockjaw: See tetanus.
Low blood pressure: Anise, Rosemary.
Low blood sugar: See hypoglycemia.
Lung congestion: Angelica, Black Pepper, Capsicum, Caraway, Celery seed, Cinnamon, Fennel, Fenugreek, Garlic, Ginger, Horseradish, Juniper, Lovage, Sage, Savory, Sunflower, Thyme, White Mustard.
Lymph glands (to cleanse): Dandelion, Ginger.

Malaria: See fevers.
Measles: Burdock, Capsicum, Fennel, Garlic, Ginger, Kelp, Oregano, Sage, Spearmint.
Memory (to improve): Angelica, Anise, Capsicum, Garlic, Ginger, Lemon Balm, Lovage.
Menopause: Lemon Balm, Rosemary.

Menstruation: Anise, Basil, Caraway, Cinnamon, Ginger, Lemon Balm, Marjoram, Oregano, Parsley, Saffron, Sage, Tarragon (*see also* female problems).

Mental-emotional disorders: Basil, Peppermint (*see also* nervous disorders).

Migraine headaches: See headaches; stress.

Milk flow: Anise.

Morning sickness: See nausea.

Motion sickness: Black Pepper, Marjoram, Oregano.

Mouth sores: Borage, Paprika, Sage (*see also* bad breath; oral hygiene).

Mucus: Black Pepper, Slippery Elm.

Mumps: Burdock, Fennel, Garlic, Ginger, Kelp, Oregano, Sage, Spearmint.

Narcotics antidote (drug addiction): Marjoram.

Nausea: Angelica, Anise, Basil, Black Pepper, Caraway, Cinnamon, Cloves, Coriander, Savory, Spearmint.

Nervous disorders: Angelica, Borage, Celery seed, Cinnamon, Lemon Balm, Marjoram, Oregano, Peppermint, Pumpkin Pie Spice, Rosemary, Sage, Savory, Spearmint, (*see also* hysteria).

Neuralgia: Black Mustard, Fenugreek, Horseradish, Peppermint (*see also* pain; paralysis; nervous disorders).

Night blindness: Annatto, Capsicum, Dandelion.

Night sweats: Sage.

Nocturnal emission (to prevent): Parsley.

Nosebleed: Kelp.

Obesity: Fennel, Kelp, Lovage, Sesame (*see also* cholesterol).

Oral hygiene: Allspice, Anise, Borage, Cinnamon, Cloves, Sage, Watercress (*see also* bad breath; toothache; tooth decay).

Oral surgery: Kelp.

Pain (with swelling): Angelica.

Pain (mild): Allspice.

Paralysis: Black Mustard, Black Pepper, Ginger, Horseradish.

Parkinson's disease: Marjoram, Sage.

Perspiration (to promote): Angelica, Bay, Borage, Ginger, Juniper, Lemon Balm, Lovage, Saffron.

Perspiration (to reduce): Sage.
Phlebitis: See varicose veins.
Piles: See hemorrhoids.
Pimples:: See blood purifiers; rash.
Placenta (to assist expulsion of): Basil, Juniper (*see also* childbirth).
Pleurisy: Borage, Lovage, White Mustard.
Pneumonia: Allspice, Black Mustard, Borage, Chili Powder, Cinnamon, Cloves, Garlic, Sunflower, White Mustard.
Poison ivy: See rash.
Poison oak: See rash.
Poisoning (heavy metal): Garlic, Kelp, liquid Chlorophyll drink, Onion, Slippery Elm.
Poisoning (Strychnine and other chemicals): Bay.
Poor breathing: Fennel.
Poor digestion: Black Pepper.
Pregnancy: Capsicum, Fenugreek, Garlic, Slippery Elm (*see also* childbirth; nausea.).
Premature birth: Sesame, Slippery Elm.
Psoriasis: See rash.
Purgatives: Allspice.
Pyorrhea: See oral hygiene.

Rabies: Curry Powder, Tarragon.
Radiation (exposure to): Kelp.
Rash (skin): Basil, Borage, Burdock, Dandelion, Lovage, Thyme, Watercress.
Recuperation: Borage, Fenugreek, Slippery Elm.
Rheumatism: Allspice, Angelica, Basil, Bay, Black Pepper, Borage, Burdock, Capsicum, Celery seed, Coriander, Crab Apple, Cumin, Dandelion, Fennel, Horseradish, Juniper, Marjoram, Peppermint, Rosemary, Spearmint, Sunflower, Thyme, Turmeric, White Mustard, (*see also* arthritis).
Rickets: See scurvy.
Ringworm: Black Pepper, Garlic, Parsley, Thyme.

Saliva (excessive flow): Sage.
Saliva (to promote flow): Capsicum, Ginger, Kelp, Savory.
Scabies: Sage.
Scalp: See hair-scalp problems.
Scar tissue: Fenugreek, Kelp, Sesame, Slippery Elm, Sunflower.

Sciatica: Black Mustard, Fenugreek, Ginger, Horseradish.

Scurvy: Angelica, Capsicum, Fenugreek, Paprika, Slippery Elm, Watercress.

Secretions (to reduce): Sage.

Semen (discharge of): See nocturnal emission.

Sexual desire (deficient): Bay, Coriander, Fenugreek, Lovage, Marjoram, Savory.

Sexual desire (excessive): Coriander, Oregano, Sage.

Shingles: Angelica.

Shock: Curry Powder, Ginger.

Shortness of breath: See breathing difficulties.

Sinusitis: Angelica, Onion.

Skin discoloration: Bay, Celery seed, Chinese Angelica, Cinnamon, Fenugreek, Lemon Balm, Slippery Elm, Thyme (*see also* bruises).

Skin disorders: Borage, Burdock, Sunflower, Thyme.

Smoking (tobacco, to stop): Fenugreek, Lemon Balm, Sunflower seeds.

Snake bites: See venomous bites.

Sore throat: Burdock, Fenugreek, Garlic, Ginger, Horseradish, Juniper, Lemon Balm, Lovage, Sage, Savory, Slippery Elm, Thyme, White Mustard (*see also* strep throat; tonsillitis).

Sores: Angelica, Annatto, Borage, Burdock, Fenugreek, Garlic, Juniper, Lemon Balm, Rosemary, Slippery Elm, Thyme.

Spasms (of muscles): Basil, Cumin, Dill, Marjoram, Sage, Spearmint.

Spleen (to stimulate): Angelica, Fennel, Sesame.

Sprains: Bay.

Staph infection: Sesame, Turmeric.

Stimulant: Capsicum, Celery seed, Peppermint.

Stomachache: See indigestion; intestinal gas.

Strep throat: Black Pepper, Borage, Capsicum, Garlic, Ginger, Horseradish, Sage, Thyme, White Mustard (*see also* tonsillitis).

Stress: Basil, Sesame.

Sumac (poison): See rash.

Sunburn: See burns.

Surgical dressing: Lemon Balm.

Syphilis: See venereal disease.

Teeth (loose): Juniper.
Tetanus: Burdock, Lovage, Thyme.
Tonsillitis: Borage, Capsicum, Fenugreek, Garlic, Ginger, Horseradish, Peppermint, Sage, Slippery Elm, White Mustard.
Toothache (and tooth decay): Allspice, Anise, Bay, Cloves, Garlic, Lemon Balm, Marjoram, Oregano, Savory, Slippery Elm, Thyme.
Tuberculosis: Angelica, Chives, Cloves, Dandelion, Slippery Elm, Thyme.
Typhoid: Angelica, Kelp, Slippery Elm.

Ulcers: Allspice, Anise, Burdock, Capsicum, Fenugreek, Garlic, Kelp, Lemon Balm, Onion, Pumpkin Pie Spice, Sage.
Urinary problems: Angelica, Basil, Borage, Burdock, Celery seed, Chives, Dandelion, Fennel, Garlic, Ginger, Horseradish, Juniper, Lemon Balm, Lovage, Parsley, Rosemary, Slippery Elm, Spearmint, Tarragon (*see also* kidney stones).

Vaginal discharge: See leucorrhea.
Vaginitis: Bay (*see also* female problems).
Varicose veins: Allspice, Capsicum, Marjoram, Saffron, Thyme, Turmeric.
Venereal disease: Angelica, Basil, Black Pepper, Burdock, Celery Seed, Juniper, Onion, Parsley, Slippery Elm, Thyme.
Venomous bites (of insects, spiders, snakes): Angelica, Basil, Borage, Curry Powder, Fennel, Garlic, Lemon Balm, Onion, Parsley, Sage, Sunflower, Tarragon.
Vertigo: Black Pepper (*see also* dizziness).
Viral infections: Cumin.
Vision (poor): See eyesight.
Vomiting (to induce): Angelica.
Vomiting (to stop): See nausea.

Warts (to remove): Dandelion, Garlic, Onion, Sage.
Weakness (general, of body): Capsicum, Chili Powder, Chives, Dandelion, Fenugreek, Garlic, Ginger, Kelp, Peppermint, Savory, Sesame, Slippery Elm, Sunflower, Watercress.

Whooping cough: Angelica, Anise, Basil, Bay, Fenugreek, Garlic, Horseradish, Oregano, Saffron, Slippery Elm, Sunflower, Thyme.

Worms (internal): Annatto, Borage, Chives, Garlic, Horseradish, Kelp, Slippery Elm, Tarragon, Thyme, Turmeric.

Wounds: Allspice, Angelica, Annatto, Burdock, Capsicum, Fenugreek, Garlic, Ginger, Juniper, Kelp, Lemon Balm, Onion, Rosemary, Slippery Elm.

PART TWO

Herbs and Spices and Their Uses

Allspice (Pimenta officinalis)
  Characteristic: Resembles a blend of Cinnamon, Nutmeg and Cloves (hence the name).
  Part used: Fruit, especially the shell.
  Applications:
    Appetite: Stimulates it. Use as tea or flavoring agent in other drinks and some foods.
    Cuts, scrapes, minor wounds: Tea has some antiseptic properties due to presence of eugenol.
    Diabetes: Lowers blood sugar.
    Digestion: Tea stimulates production of trypsin in small intestine which in turn improves the assimilation of protein taken into the body.
    Frostbite: A warm tea as a reviving agent.
    Hypothermia: Warm tea internally and warm vapors of same inhaled with towel put over head and pan of tea for covering.
    Intestinal gas: Action similar to Cloves, Mace and Nutmeg.
    Oral hygiene: Bad breath; mouthwash; tooth decay; flavoring agent in commercial toothpaste.
    Pain (mild): Tea has minor anesthetic properties due to presence of eugenol.
    Pneumonia: Warm tea internally; warm liniment with Ginger root added, to be rubbed on skin with vigorous massage; inhaled with method described under hypothermia.
    Purgatives (to assist): Moderates harsh action of *Cascara sagrada*, Buckthorn bark and Rhubarb root.
    Rheumatism: Warm tea internally; hot pack soaked in warm tea applied to sore joints and muscles.
    Ulcer: Some warm tea (1 cup) with each meal (preferably lunch and dinner).

Varicose veins (also gout and edema): Jamaicans have used the leaves of Allspice in baths of soaking solutions for varicose veins.

Non-medical uses: Allspice has antioxidant properties just as Rosemary and Sage do, and could be used in place of BHT or BHA as a preservative for some kinds of foods.

Angelica (*Angelica archangelica; Angelica officinalis*)

Characteristic: An agreeable perfume odor, comparable to musk or juniper; flavor resembles Juniper berry.

Parts used: Root, fruit, seeds.

Applications:

Alcoholism: 1/4–1 teaspoon of dried root, consumed as tea, will annul craving for alcohol.

Anemia: Fill 00 capsules with powdered herb; take 3 per day—1 with each meal.

Appetite: 1 cup mildly warm tea to increase appetite with a meal.

Arthritis (also gout and rheumatism): Tea of roots; poultice of mashed roots applied to chest.

Bad breath: Tea of roots, used as mouthwash.

Bronchitis (pneumonia): Drink tea made from roots; apply poultice of mashed roots on chest.

Cancer: Root and seeds reported to reduce tumors.

Cramps: Warm tea internally and massage afflicted area. Application of warm packs soaked in tea may also prove helpful.

Deafness: Tincture, as ear drops.

Electric shock: Warm tea internally; rub down entire body with Angelica tea in sponge; then administer light yet vigorous massage all over, with upward motions toward heart.

Epilepsy: Warm packs soaked in tea on neck, throat, forehead and chest; then cool packs soaked in *strong* Peppermint tea on same areas. Alternate until patient revives and seizure ends.

Eyesight (to improve): Make infusion of root; apply as eyedrops. Sometimes combined with Eyebright herb.

Fever: Warm tea internally; soak bedsheet in warm tea, wrap around body, then cover with heavy wool blankets to promote sweating. Give warm tea during this period.

Fungus (lungs, hands, feet)—Capsules (00) internally of powdered root (4 per day). Soak hands, feet in strong decoction of root.

Gastroenteritis: Warm tea internally flavored with a little Licorice root or powdered Cinnamon bark.

Heartburn (heart stimulant): Tea of roots, or fresh herb.

Hemorrhage: Consume tea of roots, or apply fresh herb externally.

Hives and shingles: Soothing effect on nerves of skin when used as a lotion or salve.

Hypoglycemia: Consume tea of roots or fresh herb. *CAUTION: Not recommended for diabetics.*

Indigestion: See upset stomach.

Intestinal purifier: See under Fever for more details. An enema of Angelica root tea may also be taken *occasionally*.

Lice: Powdered seeds to kill lice.

Liver (and spleen) stimulant: Consume root tea.

Lung congestion (asthma, emphysema): Consume root tea.

Memory: Equal parts of Angelica root and Peppermint leaves internally as a tea.

Nervous disorders: Tea of root or leaves is excellent tranquilizer.

Pain (with swelling): Poultice of Angelica root mixed with pounded leaves of Wormwood (*Artemesia canadensis*).

Perspiration (to promote): Tea of roots.

Scurvy: Tea of herb, used to prevent, due to high vitamin C content of leaves and stalks.

Sinusitis: Burn scrapings of dried roots; inhale vapor.

Tuberculosis: Tea of roots.

Typhoid: Tea of roots.

Upset stomach: Warm tea internally. Consume ½ to ¾ teaspoon in 1 pint of warm water.

Urinary difficulties: Tea of root.

Venereal disease: Make tea of roots, use as wash on affected part.

Venomous bites: Traditional healers use tea of roots to neutralize poisons of snakes, spiders and insects.

Vomiting (to induce): Steep root in water; consume 1 to 2 teaspoons in 1 pint of water.

Whooping cough: Consume tea of roots; apply poultice of roots on chest.

Wounds: A *strong* decoction of the root (preferably fresh) with half again as much Juniper berries used as a wash for great antiseptic value.

Non-medical uses:

Fishing and hunting: Rub fresh root onto hands and clothing to attract deer. A small amount applied to fish bait, gives off aroma that attracts fish.

Pig fodder: Improves flavor of meat to feed hogs the root.

Anise (Pimpinella anisum)

Characteristic: Sweet Licorice flavor and aroma.

Part used: Seeds.

Application:

Appetite: Tea with meal.

Asthma (bronchitis; lung congestion): Warm tea.

Bad dreams (insomnia): Aniseed is said to prevent nightmares from occurring if stuffed into pillow.

Bronchitis and chest congestion: Oil of Anise (10 drops) in 6 oz. warm water taken internally to loosen phlegm.

Cramps (to alleviate): Warm tea.

Dizziness (giddiness; vertigo): Motion sickness will be relieved by drinking some warm tea or chewing a few seeds.

Edema: Insatiable thirst quenched by chewing Aniseed.

Epilepsy: Warm tea.

Flatulence (gas): Some oil (5 drops) in 4 oz. warm water internally for relief.

Insect repellent: Oil of Aniseed mixed with oil of Sassafras applied externally.

Intestinal gas: Warm tea taken orally or rectally in an enema. Make tea with equal parts Aniseed, Caraway and Fennel.

Intestinal purifier: Tea made with equal parts Aniseed, Caraway and Fennel.

Laxative: Take with Cascara, Buckthorn or Rhubarb to make it milder on the bowels.

Lice: Salve or lotion.

Liver stimulant: Warm tea.

Low blood pressure: 4–5 capsules per day. Fill 00 gelatin size with powdered seeds. Take with or without meals.

Memory stimulant: Tea of the Aniseed has ability to exhil-
arate the mental faculties.

Milk flow (to promote): Warm tea before retiring assures
prompt milk supply.

Menstruation (to promote): Warm tea.

Oral hygiene (bad breath; tooth decay): Gargle with
tincture; apply cotton soaked with oil of Aniseed to
cavities.

Ulcer: Capsule (4 per day); tea (1–2 cups); or just chew
some of the whole seeds. Flavored saliva will coat and
heal stomach sores.

Vomiting (to prevent): Warm tea.

Whooping cough (hiccoughs; smoker's cough): Gargle with tea.

Non-medical uses: Seeds used as mouse trap bait. Pigeon bait
for removing unwanted birds (it is poisonous to them).

Annatto (Bixa orellana)

Characteristic: Yellowish-red dyestuff with slightly pungent,
acrid flavor.

Part used: The pulp around the seeds.

Applications:

Infection: Increases resistance of young children to viruses;
mix with liquid drinks such as eggnog, carrot juice, etc.

Intestinal worms: Equal parts of powdered Tobacco leaves
with Annatto as tea; also used externally for vermin and
chiggers.

Liver tonic: Useful in raw vegetable juices designed for the
liver.

Night blindness: Add to Dandelion blossoms in blender
and consume as a beverage. Combined with a little water
or liquid chlorophyll to make a liquid; add one of the
sweeter spices for flavor.

Wounds: Apply externally in powdered form. 1 part Annatto to 3 parts Goldenseal root to enhance activity of
Goldenseal.

Basil (Ocimum basilicum)

Characteristic: Aromatic-like Mint and mildly-flavored like
Licorice.

Part used: Herb.

Applications:

Antiseptic aerosol: Burn Basil as incense in rooms of the sick.

Breast milk (to promote): As a tea or used in food as a general spice. Works best with soup.

Childbirth (pains of): As a tea several days before labor begins.

Constipation: Cool tea.

Ear (inflammation of): Warm tincture or expressed juice of fresh Basil leaves poured directly into the ear.

Headache: 1 cup tea taken internally.

Indigestion (gastroenteritis): Tea with meals.

Infection: Tea internally. And used externally as a wash. Also valuable as an inhalant (see first entry above).

Insect stings (venomous bites): Apply fresh leaves to area of bite.

Menstruation (to promote): Hot tea.

Mental and emotional disorders: Warm tea. Often has a pleasant, calming effect if some Cinnamon, Fennel and a drop or two of Bay oil are added.

Placenta (to assist expulsion of): Several cups of tea just prior to delivery.

Poison ivy (rash): Crushed fresh leaves or salve; apply on the skin.

Rheumatism: Warm tea drunk several times per day.

Snake bites (venomous bites): Apply fresh leaves to area of bite.

Spasms (muscles and stomach): As a tea.

Stress: As a beverage several times daily; serve lukewarm.

Urine (burning, scalding): Warm tea several times daily.

Veneral disease: An infusion orally and as a douche.

Vomiting (nausea): Warm tea.

Whooping cough: Warm tea consumed slowly; also as a gargle.

Non-medical uses:

Organic gardening: Plant wherever animal fertilizer is used; will keep down barnyard odor.

Insecticide: Prepare strong decoction and spray on cabbage and tomato plants.

Bay (Laurus nobilis)
    Characteristic: Forest aroma; pleasantly bitter.
    Parts used: Leaves, fruit, oil.
    Applications:
        Coma: 3–4 cups of warm tea can often reverse this condition.
        Cramps: Warm tea.
        Dandruff: Tea as a hair rinse.
        Deafness: Same procedure as for earache.
        Earache: One or two drops of extracted oil into the ear.
        Fungus (toenails, fingernails): Soak hands or feet in strong solution of Bay decoction.
        High blood pressure: 1 cup tea or 2 capsules (00) powder internally.
        Hysteria: Tea made of leaves and berries acts as a sedative.
        Indigestion: Tea with meals.
        Perspiration (to promote): Warm tea used as internal cleanser in modest amounts.
        Poisoning (strychnine and other chemicals): 3–5 cups of cool tea to prevent lethal convulsions and death.
        Rheumatism: Extracted oil or tincture applied externally; action improved when used with heat.
        Sexual stimulant: Tea made of leaves purportedly increases secretion of semen in men, according to Sanskrit writers.
        Sprains (bruises): Oil applied externally.
        Toothache: Apply oil to cotton and place on side of cavity.
        Vaginitis and uterine infection: Douche made of strong decoction of Bay.
        Whooping cough: Warm tea.
    Non-medical uses:
        Insecticide: The leaves are used to drive away fleas and lice, and when placed in cannisters will prevent moths and bugs in flour and cereals.
        Good for wheat storage in place of dry ice.

Black pepper (Piper nigrum)
    Characteristic: Slightly acrid taste; somewhat pungent odor.
    Parts used: Dried, unripe fruit.
    Applications:
        Abortion: Varying quantities of tea drunk in East Africa during first 2 months to expel developing fetus. NOT RECOMMENDED WITHOUT MEDICAL SUPERVISION!

Aperients (to assist): Enhances the medicinal properties of Boneset, Borage, Burdock, Dandelion, Elder and Couchgrass.

Appetite: See under poor digestion.

Arthritis: Tea used daily (1–2 cups) produces gradual and beneficial changes.

Coma: Warm tea internally.

Fever: Hot (black) Pepper tea made with dried Peppercorns taken internally to promote sweating. Use in weakness following fevers. Valuable in malarial fever to prevent it from recurring.

Intestinal mucus: Use as a tea or enema.

Migraine headaches: As a tea: 1 part Pepper to 3 parts Cinnamon.

Motion sickness (air, sea, land): Tea internally.

Mucus: Gargle tea for mucus in the throat; warm tea for lung congestion.

Nausea: Prevents it; use as a tea.

Paralysis (temporary): As a tea for temporary paralysis of tongue or jaws.

Poor digestion: Tea promotes production of hydrochloric acid.

Rheumatism: See under arthritis.

Ringworm (lice): Tea in strong solution as a wash for scalp.

Strep throat: Gargle with hot tea with lemon juice added.

Venereal disease: Warm tea as a douche.

Vertigo: Cool tea taken internally.

Non-medical uses:

Powerful insecticide against boll weevils, household pests and agricultural insects.

Borage (Borago officinalis)

Characteristic: The fresh herb has a cucumber-like fragrance and faint flavor.

Parts used: Leaves and flowers.

Applications:

Breast milk (to increase): As a tea, twice daily.

Eye inflammation: Cool tea on cloth, apply to eye.

Fevers: Warm tea.

Gastroenteritis: Cool tea with a meal.

Heart stimulant: Warm tea in between meals and before exercising.

Insect stings (venomous bites): Warm tea internally; and locally as a poultice.

Intestinal worms: Warm tea.

Jaundice: Use as a tea.

Mild nervousness: Warm tea.

Mouth sores (strep throat; tonsillitis): Warm tea as a gargle.

Perspiration (to promote): Warm tea promotes abundant sweating. Cool tea internally, and applied as poultice on forehead, neck, throat and chest will help to reduce a fever within minutes.

Pleurisy: Warm tea.

Pneumonia (influenza; lung congestion): Warm tea.

Recuperation: 2–3 cups tea sipped slowly throughout the day.

Rheumatism: 1–2 cups tea per day.

Skin disorders: An external wash is made of the tea for scabs, sores and psoriasis.

Snake bites (venomous bites): Warm tea internally; poultices externally.

Tonic (blood purifier): Tea good for those recovering from lengthy illnesses; also used with cleansing programs.

Urination (to promote): Tea.

Non-medical uses:

Sprigs of Borage added during brewing improve flavor of beer.

Burdock *(Arctium lappa)*

Characteristic: Sweet, mucilaginous taste to the root. When the stalks are cut and boiled, they yield a taste similar to cooked asparagus.

Parts used: Root, leaves, seeds.

Applications:

Allergies: 6 capsules/tablets per day; or 2 cups tea in between meals per day.

Blood purifier: Tea of root.

Boils (carbuncles): Tea of root internally; also as poultice.

Burns: (Open wounds and sores; hemorrhoids): Salve made of the root, leaves or seeds.

Childbirth: Tea of root taken one week prior to delivery.

Edema (dropsy): Seeds as tea to eliminate water retention.

Eye infection: Tea made of equal parts Burdock root and Eyebright herb. Use as an eyewash 3–4 times per day.

Gout (swellings): Leaves as poultice.

Hair loss: Rinse hair with tea, massaging scalp vigorously at same time. Leave in hair for about 5 minutes before rinsing tea out.

Hysteria: Tea of seeds to calm excited nerves.

Kidney stones: Decoction of seeds.

Liver stimulant: 4 capsules/tablets per day as supplement; or 1 cup tea daily.

Plant rash: Freshly-crushed leaves antidote for Stinging Nettle, and mild cases of Poison Ivy, Oak or Sumac rash.

Rheumatism: Tea of root.

Skin disorders: Tea of root internally, or externally as a wash, for eczema, psoriasis, acne, leprosy and eruptive disorders like measles, mumps, chicken pox.

Sore throat: Gargle with strong decoction of root tea. Mildly effective.

Tetanus: Tea of root or seeds.

Ulcer (external on legs, etc.): Wash sores with strong decoction of root.

Ulcer (stomach): Root tea or capsules each day.

Urinary problems: Tea made of 1 part Juniper berries with 3 parts Burdock root. Drink 2–3 cups daily. Or 1 capsule of Juniper with 3 capsules of Burdock root in between meals, with an 8 oz. glass of liquid.

Venereal disease: Root or seeds in tea/douche form.

Capsicum [*Cayenne pepper*] (*Capsicum frutescens; Capsicum annuum*)
Characteristic: Pungent, burning taste.
Part used: The fruit.
Applications:

Note: Ginger root may be substituted in the place of Capsicum for those who cannot tolerate the latter.

Appetite: Use on food in powdered form out of a shaker wherever Black pepper would be used. Or take 1 capsule with meal or tomato juice to stimulate appetite and avoid burning sensation.

Arthritis: 2 capsules per day or use on food to improve blood circulation and reduce tissue inflammation, both common in arthritis.

Atherosclerosis: Daily modest intake of Capsicum along with Garlic will greatly reduce this problem or keep it from occurring.

Backache: Tinctures of Cayenne and Peppermint applied on area of soreness and massaged into the skin will give great relief in most cases.

Blood circulation (to improve): See above first 2 entries.

Blood clotting (to prevent): See above first 3 entries.

Cancer: Only of value in certain formulations to expedite their transfer throughout the body. Has definite limitations with certain kinds of cancers, such as cancer of the colon for instance. Not recommended at all with chemotherapy.

Chickenpox: Valuable in breaking a fever and increasing elimination. Children (ages 6–10): 1 capsule daily with food or tomato juice. Youth (ages 11–18): 1–3 capsules daily with food or tomato juice (amount can be increased with age if needed). Adults: Use according to needs and body tolerance for such.

Colitis: Very small amounts may stop bleeding: but it is *strongly* recommended to be used with Fenugreek or Slippery Elm bark in larger dose for this.

Common cold: Hot chicken soup laced with Cayenne and Garlic should knock the common cold for good.

Cramps: Valuable internally to increase flow of blood to muscles.

Emaciation: As a food condiment and means of mild nourishment.

Emphysema: Some Cayenne in hot soup, water, or other clear liquid suitable to take with this spice, will usually stimulate the lungs more and increase respiratory activity.

Heart stimulant: See under atherosclerosis.

Indigestion: Only recommended if problem is due to *lack* of hydrochloric acid in stomach. *NOT* recommended otherwise if problem is caused by an irritant of some sort. Use Peppermint or Fennel instead.

Influenza: See under common cold.

Intestinal mucus: See under emphysema. Taken in such a form will usually cut mucus quite well.

Lung congestion: See under emphysema.

Measles: See under chickenpox. Also promotes sweating in some cases.

Memory: Increases flow of blood, which in turn delivers more oxygen to the brain.

Night blindness: Taken in conjunction with Dandelion *flowers* (fresh) in salad form or mixed up as a "green drink" with a little liquid chlorophyll may help the eyes to produce "visual purple" which solves this problem.

Pregnancy: *Modest* use of this in food and drink or 1–2 capsules per day with meal or tomato juice throughout 9-month gestation period is recommended.

Rheumatism: See under arthritis.

Saliva: Sipping tomato juice which has been laced with some Capsicum and holding it momentarily in the mouth before swallowing or swishing it around inside, will induce the saliva glands to produce more of their substance, which helps improve the overall condition of the stomach in general.

Scurvy: Adding Capsicum to certain food dishes will correct *mild* forms of scurvy in most cases.

Stimulant (carrier): Improves overall tone of the system and acts as transport for delivering other herbs more quickly throughout the body.

Strep throat: Gargle with relatively warm water to which has been added some Capsicum and lemon juice. NOTE: Capsicum *definitely* enhances the overall medicinal and nutritional activity of vitamin C or ascorbic acid. To every 3 tablets of vitamin C, at least 1 capsule of Capsicum or Ginger root should be taken for maximum effectiveness and assimilation of the C.

Tonsillitis: See strep throat.

Ulcer (stomach): Numerous people have benefited from ingesting the species of Cayenne known as *Capsicum annuum*. But it should be pointed out, that this doesn't always hold true for another species, *C. frutescens* or African Bird-pepper, which is much hotter and has been clinically known to induce, if not aggravate, ulcers already present. *C. annuum* is a lighter reddish-orange, while *C. frutescens* is much darker in color. *C. annuum* is

in the 40,000–60,000 BTU range, while *C. frutescens* is
generally much higher—80,000–100,000 BTUs.

Varicose veins: See under blood circulation. DO NOT APPLY
EXTERNALLY—will burn the skin!

Weakness: See various listings under chickenpox, common
cold, emaciation, etc.

Wounds: Powdered Capsicum sprinkled into a wound or
applied as a poultice to an open and bleeding wound
will generally stop the bleeding within a matter of minutes. And it doesn't really sting either. Kelp may also be
used for this, either with or in place of Capsicum with
equal results.

Caraway (Carum carvi)

Characteristic: The leaves and roots are delicately flavored;
seeds are pungent.

Parts used: Fruit, seeds, leaves, root.

Applications:

Appetite: Chewing a few seeds prior to a meal will stimulate it.

Bad breath (halitosis): Gargle and mouthwash made with
tea.

Breast milk: 2 cups of tea per day will usually stimulate
flow of milk.

Chemotherapy: A broth or tea made of Slippery Elm bark
and a few Caraway seeds, and taken regularly *before and
after* chemotherapy will generally allay much of the nausea accompanying such treatments later on.

Diarrhea: As a tea.

Female problems: Tea promotes menstruation; relieves uterine cramps; promotes breast milk.

Flavoring for bitter herbs: Makes Valerian, Wormwood
and Goldenseal more tolerable.

Lung congestion (breathing difficulties; bronchitis; asthma):
Tea serves as a mild expectorant.

Nausea (vomiting): Tea is antidote for herbal side effects
(such as caused by Lobelia).

Shortness of breath (to prevent): Good to take when jog-
ging, running, mountain climbing, etc.

Cardamom *(Elettaria cardamomum)*
  Characteristic: Mild, pleasant Ginger flavor.
  Part used: Dried, ripe seeds.
  Applications:
    Adjuvant for other herbs: Enhances the performance of Angelica, Lemon balm, Wood betony, Coriander, Chickweed, Parsley, Sarsaparilla, Wormwood, Thyme, etc.
    Bad breath: Chew a few seeds.
    Flavoring agent for other herbs: Improves taste of Valerian, Wormwood, Skunk cabbage, etc.
    Indigestion (heartburn): As a tea; or chew some seeds.
    Intestinal gas (heartburn): As a tea; also reduces gas caused by garlic.
    Minor headaches: Warm tea.

Celery seed *(Apium graveolens)*
  Characteristic: Aromatic odor and taste.
  Part used: The seeds.
  Applications:
    Appetite: Tea sipped slowly will improve it.
    Bruises: Hot packs soaked in Peppermint tea and cold packs soaked in Celery seed tea, and applied alternately, will reduce swellings and minimize skin discolorations.
    Gout: Celery seed tea increases urination.
    Hives: Tea internally.
    Hysteria: Tea.
    Insomnia: Warm tea one hour before retiring.
    Kidney stones: 3–4 cups tea daily.
    Lung congestion: Warm tea flavored with a little Peppermint oil internally.
    Nervousness (hyperactivity): Equal parts of Celery seed and Skullcap as tea.
    Rheumatism: As a tea mixed with Damiana.
    Skin discoloration: See under bruises.
    Stimulant: Strong tea in morning.
    Urination (to promote): Tea.
    Venereal disease: Used as an external wash or internal douche relieves itching rash.

Chili powder *(Blend)*
  Characteristic: Spicy and hot.

Herbs used: Chili peppers, Cumin, Oregano, Salt, Garlic.
Applications:
  Fever: Soup or broth.
  Frostbite (hypothermia; severe cold): Warm or hot soup, broth.
  Heart attack: Soup, broth, or tea (warm) internally. Hot poultices on bottoms of feet and hands and back of neck and spine. DO NOT LEAVE FOR VERY LONG lest it burn the skin.
  Influenza (common cold): Soup or broth.
  Pneumonia: Warm soup or broth.
  Weakness: Soup or broth taken moderately.

Chinese Angelica; Tang kuei; Dong guei (Angelica sinensis)
  Characteristic: The root contains a highly aromatic oil.
  Part used: Root.

  Note: Tang kuei can promote further bleeding in women who hemorrhage easily during menstruation. Does not affect all women this way, however, *only* a few.

Applications:
  Alcoholism: Tea of equal parts of roots and Peach bark.
  Arthritis: Tea of roots.
  Bronchitis: Tea of roots.
  Chemotherapy (against side effects): Tea of roots.
  Childbirth (to ease): Commence drinking tea of roots, two months prior to expected delivery.
  Cirrhosis of the liver: Cool tea 3 times daily.
  Constipation: Tea of roots.
  Esophagus (cancer of): Warm tea will give some relief; allow food to be swallowed if taken with meals.
  Female disorders (menopause, hot flashes, menstruation): Tea of roots. See cautionary note above.
  Fevers: Tea of roots.
  Headache: Capsules (2–3) or tea (1 cup) internally; warm pack soaked in tea on forehead, too.
  Intestinal pain: Tea of roots.
  Skin discoloration (black-and-blue marks): Hot and cold packs of infusion made from roots.

Note: There is only one source in the United States for the purchase of Chinese Angelica, and that is through a firm licensed to export it by the Chinese Government. The address for ordering, which should mention the Chinese name *Tang kuei* is: Hong Ning Company, 827 North Broadway, Los Angeles, California 90012.

Chives (Allium schoenoprasum)
   Characteristic: Delicate onion flavor.
   Part used: The stalks.
   Applications:
      Abortion (to prevent): The diosgenin in Chives can be converted by the body into the female hormone progesterone, which has been used clinically to stop uterine hemorrhaging and threatened abortions.
      Anemia: Eaten fresh in salads or other food dishes.
      Cholesterol (to reduce): Aides in the digestion of fatty foods; reduces serum cholesterol in blood.
      Intestinal mucus: Use fresh. Chew a stalk slowly. Allow aroma to penetrate down into throat and lungs.
      Tuberculosis: See above.
      Urinary problems: Eat fresh. Promotes urination.
      Weakness: Use fresh with food. Good tonic effect on system.
      Worms: Consumed fresh or as a simple clear broth.

Cinnamon (Cinnamomum zeylanicum)
   Characteristic: Warm, spicy flavor.
   Part used: Bark.
   Applications:
      Bruises: Apply poultice of paste made with equal parts Cinnamon and Turmeric.
      Diarrhea: Mix one teaspoon Cinnamon to eight ounces of water, milk or other liquid. Take every 2–4 hours until diarrhea is corrected. One teaspoon each of Slippery Elm and Cinnamon works even better.
      Fainting spells: Warm tea as a stimulant.
      Indigestion: Tea; or add powder to a liquid.
      Internal bleeding: Useful hemostatic for menstrual or ulcer hemorrhage. Use as a warm tea; or add powder to appropriate liquid form.
      Intestinal gas: Warm tea; or powder in liquid drink.

Lung congestion (bronchitis; coughs; pneumonia): Warm tea is useful in the early stage of respiratory problems.

Menstruation (female problems): Use in tea or douche form.

Nausea (vomiting): Cinnamon bark tea or Cinnamon in warm milk corrects nausea motion and extreme altitude sickness.

Nervousness: Warm tea; or powder in warm milk or herb tea like Chamomile; has a sedative effect.

Oral hygiene: Dental antiseptic for gum disease, mouth sores, cankers and cavities. Used in powder form on wet toothbrush regularly. Mix equal parts of White Oak bark and Cinnamon for similar results.

Skin discoloration: See bruises.

Skin fungus: The East Indian name for Cinnamon is Dalchini. It is used as a wash and soaking agent for skin fungus.

Cloves (Eugenia caryophyllata; Caryophyllus aromaticus; Syzygium aromaticum)

Characteristic: Hot, spicy and penetrating.

Part used: The embryo seed in undeveloped flowers.

Applications:

Diarrhea: Warm tea.

Earache: Warm Clove oil; place a few drops in ear canal and cover with flannel cloth.

Nausea (vomiting): Warm tea. Antidote for side effects of Lobelia.

Oral hygiene: Oil or as powder; good for tooth decay and pain.

Toothache: Warm oil soaked on cotton; apply directly to site of pain.

Tuberculosis (bronchitis and pneumonia): Warm tea.

Coriander (Coriandrum sativum)

Characteristic: Pleasant lemon-orange flavor.

Parts used: Fruit, seed and fresh leaves.

Applications:

Adjuvant for purgatives: Modifies the griping action of Cascara, Buckthorn and Rhubarb.

Antidote for strong herbs: Prevents unpleasant side effects of Scammony, Lobelia, Mayapple, Senna and Belladonna.

Appetite: Tea.

Arthritis: Tea.

Cholesterol (to reduce): Take as a tea with meals, especially those with meat.

Cramps: Tea.

Diabetes: Tea gives mild action to help lower high blood sugar level.

Diarrhea: For acute and chronic diarrhea, use the following formula:

½ oz. or 2 tablespoons Allspice, ½ oz. Cinnamon, ⅛ oz. Coriander, ¼ oz. Cloves, and ¼ oz. White Oak bark in powdered form.

In 1½ pints water, simmer down to ½ pint. Strain; then add 4 oz. honey. Bring to the boiling point again to melt honey. Then add half as much good quality brandy as there is of the syrup.

Doses: from 1 teaspoon to 2 tablespoons, 3–6 times per day according to severity of symptoms. Generally ½ to 1 teaspoon for infants; 2 tablespoons for adults.

Gout: Tea.

Heart Stimulant: Tea.

Inflammation: Tea (internal). Warm pack soaked in tea (external application).

Intestinal gas: Tea.

Nausea: Cool tea.

Rheumatism: Tea.

Sexual desire: Warm tea (internal). Warm pack soaked in tea and laid upon reproductive organs and abdomen (external application).

Crab Apple (Pyrus malus; Malus communis)

Characteristic: Austere taste due to the slightly bitter, acidic juice.

Parts used: Fruit, seeds and rootbark.

Applications:

Blood purifier: As a tea.

Cholesterol (to lower): Consume with any kind of fatty meats.

Rheumatism: Apply poultice of crushed Crab apple externally.

Cumin (Cuminum cyminum)

  Characteristic: Warm, salty-sweet; reminiscent of Caraway.

  Part used: Ripened fruit seed.

  Applications

    Abdominal spasms: Warm tea; also used in veterinary medicine.

    Intestinal gas: As a tea.

    Rheumatism—arthritis: Fresh leaves are crushed and rubbed on swollen, painful joints.

    Viral infections: Tea of seeds is strongly anti-viral due to presence of active constituents like thymol and cuminic aldehyde.

Curry Powder (Blend)

  Characteristic: Pungent and spicy.

    Herbs used: Bay, Black Pepper, Cloves, Coriander, Cumin, Fenugreek, Ginger, Nutmeg, Onion, Red Pepper, Turmeric.

  Applications:

    Electric shock, epileptic seizures, heart attack, poisonous venom, rabies and traumatic shock.

    In all of the above cases, *no food should be consumed* until conditions are past. Fasting is best. Evacuate already-consumed food with olive oil, nothing else. Administer liquid broth of Curry powder every half-hour to hour in 1 cup amounts. Repeat as necessary. OBSERVE OUTWARD PHYSIOLOGICAL SIGNS CAREFULLY (i.e., pulse, rate of breathing, color in cheeks, etc.). Seek immediate medical treatment.

Dandelion (Taraxacum officinale)

  Characteristic: Leaves and flowers are acrid and bitter; root has a robust, coffee-like flavor.

  Parts used: The leaves, flowers and root.

  Applications:

    Anemia: Use fresh in salads or tea or green drink (leaves and flower). Also in capsule or tablet form (4 per day).

    Appetite: Tea.

    Asthma: Make a "tobacco" mixture of equal parts of Dandelion root, Coltsfoot leaves and Rosemary; smoke in a pipe very slowly.

Blood purifier: Tea or capsule (root or fresh leaves and flower).

Constipation: Tea of root. Used in enema for cancer treatment, Dandelion will stimulate the liver, spleen and pancreas.

Diabetes: Tea or capsule (root).

Digestive disorders (indigestion): Strong decoction of the root 3–4 times per day.

Edema (water retention; dropsy): Strong tea of root.

Fungus: Tea or capsule (internal): Wash or soak in strong root decoction.

Gallstones (kidney stones): Strong tea of the root.

Insomnia (mild): Warm tea ½ hour before retiring.

Liver problems (jaundice; cirrhosis due to alcoholism): Tea of root in large quantities.

Lymphatic cleanser: As a tea.

Night blindness: Dandelion flowers and vitamin B6 in a liquid drink.

Rash: See fungus.

Rheumatism: Tea (internal); warm pack soaked in root decoction (external).

Tuberculosis: Strong decoction of the root several times per day.

Urination (to promote): Tea of root.

Warts (corns): The white milky latex from fresh plants is applied often to remove most warts.

Weakness: Tea or capsule or consume fresh in salad, soup or green drink.

Dill (Anethum graveolens; Peucedanum graveolens)

Characteristic: Aromatic, somewhat like Caraway, but milder and sweeter.

Part used: Dried, ripe fruit.

Applications:

Abdominal spasms (cramps): Tea.

Appetite: Use in certain foods to increase their appeal and tastiness.

Bad breath: Chew some seeds.

Breast milk (to promote): As a tea with Anise, Coriander, Fennel or Caraway.

Infant colic: Weak Dill tea in a bottle.

Insomnia: Warm tea before retiring.
Intestinal gas (indigestion): Tea.
Lice: Wash skin or hair with strong decoction.
Minor headache (stomachache): Warm tea.

Fennel (Foeniculum vulgare)
  Characteristic: Pleasant Licorice flavor, somewhat like Anise.
  Parts used: Seeds, leaves and root.
  Applications:
    Abdominal cramps: Warm tea.
    Adjuvant for other herbs: Prevents cramping caused by laxative herbs like Cascara, Buckthorn and Rhubarb. Prevents side effects of Licorice.
    Appetite (poor): Warm tea.
    Arthritis (rheumatism): Oil may be rubbed on swollen painful joints. However, too much can cause a white discoloration of the skin surrounded by dark-brown pigments (photodermatitis).
    Bad breath: Chew some of the seeds.
    Bedwetting: Warm tea. Small doses for children; larger ones for adults.
    Breast milk (to promote): 10–12 drops of tincture; also, a tea is made of the seeds, and a little barley added.
    Coughing (hoarseness): Gargle with decoction.
    Eye inflammation (eyestrain): Wash made from decoction of seeds.
    Food poisoning: Several cups of tea as an antidote.
    Gangrene: Wash area externally with strong decoction of seeds and root.
    Gout: Warm tea.
    Headache: Tea.
    Influenza: Tea.
    Intestinal purifier: Tea or enema.
    Leprosy: Tea (internal) or as a skin wash (external).
    Lung congestion: Warm tea.
    Measles: Warm tea.
    Mumps: Tea.
    Obesity: As a tea.
    Poor breathing: Warm tea.
    Stimulant for liver, spleen and gallbladder: Warm tea several times per day.

Urination (to promote): As a tea.

Venomous bites: Cool tea (internal) and hot/cold packs soaked in strong decoction and applied to neck and forehead.

Non-medical uses:

Fennel powder makes an ideal flea-and-tick medicine for dogs, cats, sheep and cattle. Apply generously on them. Or make a collar for your cat or dog stuffed with dried Fennel, Pennyroyal and Thyme leaves.

Fenugreek (Trigonella foenum graecum)

Characteristic: A bitter, peculiar taste and aroma, similar to Lovage or Celery.

Part used: The seeds.

Applications:

Appendicitis: Tea (alone or combined with Slippery Elm). Drink frequently until cleared up.

Blood clotting: Tea.

Bruises: Poultice.

Cholesterol: Drink tea with meals consisting of heavy, fatty foods.

Cod-liver oil substitute: May be used in place of cod-liver oil for tuberculosis of bone or lymph glands, rickets, anemia and general constitutional weakness following major illness.

Colitis: Tea.

Diabetes: To ¾ amount of insulin injected, take ¼ Fenugreek tea *orally*.

Fevers (malaria; yellow; typhoid; rocky mountain spotted): As a tea, considered to be equal in strength to quinine.

Gout (neuralgia; sciatica; wounds; sores): Poultice of pulverized seeds.

Hives: Tea (internal), poultice or skin wash (external).

Hoarseness: Gargle with tea.

Inflammation: Tea (internal); poultice (external).

Leucorrhea: Vaginal douche.

Lung congestion: Warm tea.

Neuralgia: Poultice.

Pregnancy (to promote): Fenugreek seeds contain substantial coumarin, which manifests estrogenic properties. Drink one cup each day during periods of sexual activity.

Scar tissue: Tea (internal) or poultice (external). Good only
if used in early stages of recent surgery before scar tissue
has a chance to form.

Scurvy: Tea.

Sexual desire: Tea.

Skin discoloration: Poultice.

Smoking: See sore throat.

Sore throat: Tea (internal) and gargle with tea.

Ulcer: Lukewarm tea.

Whooping cough: Lukewarm tea sipped very slowly.

Garlic (Allium sativum)

Characteristic: Intensely pungent; onion-like, only stronger.

Part used: Bulb (fresh).

Applications:

Antibiotic—herbal immunization: The Greek historian, He-
rodotus, mentioned that ancient Egyptians fed the Children of Israel large amounts of Garlic, Onions and
Radishes, in order to keep them fit and healthy to build
the Great Pyramid of Cheops. Very few of the children
became sick, although their Egyptian taskmasters and
rulers suffered a number of infectious disorders, including certain forms of cancer.

Appetite: Use as a food condiment.

Asthma: Boil six Cloves in apple-cider vinegar until soft;
then add one teaspoon honey or genuine maple syrup
and continue boiling on low heat until a syrup has
formed. Take as often as necessary.

Bubonic plague: Generous amounts of Garlic in the diet
each day, raises resistance to many infectious diseases.

Cancer: 6 capsules or more per day; frequent Garlic enemas.

Chickenpox: Broth or clear soup prepared with Garlic clove.

Cholesterol (to lower): Several capsules per day.

Corns (bunions; calluses; warts): Mashed Garlic on the
feet.

Diabetes: Garlic can lower blood sugar levels significantly.
Several capsules per day.

Diarrhea: Garlic enema.

Earache (ear infection): Drop some warm Garlic oil into the
ear canal; cover with flannel to keep warm overnight.
Use about 10–12 drops according to the age of the pa-

tient. Use a secondary source for warming, such as a double-boiler, or else put some Garlic oil in a jar and place in a pan of hot water for several minutes to warm.

Edema (water retention; dropsy): The oil or powder.

Electric shock: Warm broth or clear soup laced with Cayenne pepper and Garlic given internally.

Epidemics: Garlic broth, 10–12 Garlic oil capsules, frequent Garlic enemas.

Epileptic seizures: Garlic tea before and after every meal.

Fainting: Raw Garlic clove held close to the nostrils. Garlic poultices on bottom of feet.

Female problems: Vaginal douche for yeast infection.

Fevers: As broth or soup.

Gallbladder: Garlic enemas for infections and to stimulate bladder.

Gangrene (festering wounds; open sores): Fresh or powdered Kelp and Irish moss, soaked in Garlic juice, or mixed with powdered or finely chopped Garlic and applied directly upon the site of mortified tissue will assist healing.

Gastroenteritis: Garlic broth or clear soup if inflammation is due to infection. Otherwise do not use.

Heart attack (coronary arrest; myocardial infarction): Several Garlic oil capsules each day may help prevent a second or third heart attack after the first one. Fresh Garlic clove or the encapsulated oil will reduce inflammation of the heart, and permit better circulation of the blood.

Heart stimulant: See heart attack.

Hypertension (high blood pressure): The sulphur and manganese content in Garlic cloves helps to arrest this common disease.

Infection: Garlic oil capsules; Garlic broth or soup; frequent Garlic enemas.

Inflammation: Garlic oil rubbed on skin that is inflamed to prevent infections from occurring.

Influenza: See under infection.

Intestinal purifier: Garlic enema and Garlic oil capsules taken orally.

Lead and mercury poisoning: Garlic oil capsules (internal).

Leprosy: Garlic oil capsules (internal) and Garlic oil applied externally.

Liver stimulant: Garlic oil capsules.

Lung congestion (breathing difficulties; bronchitis; common cold; emphysema, hiccoughs. hoarseness): Garlic tea or oil taken internally.

Measles: Garlic oil capsules and Garlic broth or soup; Garlic enemas.

Memory: Garlic oil capsules.

Mumps: See measles.

Pneumonia: Besides internal administration, rub Garlic oil on the chest and spine.

Pregnancy: Vaginal douche of Garlic to prevent uterine infection.

Ringworm: Garlic oil capsules.

Sore throat: Garlic oil capsules and/or Garlic broth or soup.

Strep throat and tonsillitis: See sore throat.

Toothache: Raw clove, crushed, and inserted into mouth by side of pain. Keep there for 6 hours before changing.

Ulcer (external): Wash frequently with strong garlic solution.

Urinary problems: Broth.

Venomous bites (scorpion stings): Fresh Garlic cloves applied directly to the site of injury.

Weakness: Broth.

Whooping cough: See sore throat.

Worms: Garlic oil capsules (internal).

Non-medical uses:

Insecticide: Soak three ounces of chopped cloves in two teaspoons of mineral oil for 24 hours. Then slowly add 1 pint water in which ¾ of an ounce of Palmolive soap has been dissolved; stir well. Strain through fine gauze; but don't store in metallic containers. Start out with 1 part to 20 parts water, and decrease if necessary to 1 part to 100.

Ginger (Zingiber officinale)

Characteristic: Aromatic, sweet-spicy; and very penetrating.

Part used: The root.

Applications:

Abdominal cramps: Equal parts of Ginger and Hop tea.

Blood circulation: Warm tea.

Blood clot: Powdered Ginger (capsules) or Ginger tea.

Capsicum substitute: Action similar to Cayenne pepper.

Chest (heart pains): Tea.

Chickenpox: Warm Ginger tea.

Colitis: Ginger tea, capsules, or warm Ginger enema.

Diarrhea: As a tea.

Headache: 1 cup cool tea.

Heart attack: Warm Ginger tea.

Hypoglycemia: Generally 3–5 capsules a day without Licorice; 2 per day with Licorice.

Indigestion: Capsules or tea.

Infection: Capsules, tea or enema.

Laryngitis: Hot Ginger tea with honey and lemon juice.

Lung congestion (asthma; bronchitis; common cold; cough; hoarseness; influenza): Warm tea.

Lymph gland cleanser: As a tea.

Measles: Tea, capsules or enema.

Menstruation (to promote): Warm tea.

Mild paralysis (shock): Chew a little of the grated root for mouth and tongue paralysis.

Mumps: See measles.

Perspiration (to promote): Warm tea.

Saliva: Stimulates the flow of it; good for digestive disorders.

Sciatica: Warm tea. Rubdown with Ginger oil. Warm Ginger packs on site of pain and stiffness.

Strep throat (sore throat; tonsillitis): Chew the rootstock.

Urination (to promote): Tea.

Weakness: Warm tea or capsules.

Wounds: Wash with Ginger tea. Take capsules internally.

Horseradish (Cochlearia armoracia, Armoracia lapathifolia, Raphanus rusticanus, Radicula armoracia)

Characteristic: Intensely acrid and pungent.

Part used: The root.

Applications:

Appetite: Use sparingly as a food condiment. Use a pinch with apple cider vinegar to promote appetite.

Digestive disorders (indigestion): When eating oily fish or fatty meat, use Horseradish by itself or steeped in apple cider vinegar.

Edema (water retention): One ounce root and ½ ounce

Mustard seed in one pint boiling water. Let stand for 4 hours; strain. ½ cup, 3–4 times per day.

Gout: See edema.

Infection: Mix 5 tablespoons of grated Horseradish with brandy, adding a little fructose for flavor. Take 2 teaspoons every 4 hours or so until infection clears up.

Intestinal worms: Warm tea, or food condiment.

Kidney stones: Warm tea.

Liver stimulant: Root juice and honey.

Lung congestion (asthma; cough): Warm tea.

Minor paralysis: Apply poultice on external sites.

Neuralgia: Follow directions for paralysis and rheumatism.

Rheumatism—arthritis: Warm tea. May also be used externally.

Sciatica: Apply as poultice.

Sore throat (hoarseness; laryngitis; strep; tonsillitis): Warm tea as a gargle.

Urination (to promote): Tea.

Whooping cough: See under infection. Take in small amounts. Let it trickle down throat very slowly.

Juniper (*Juniperis communis*)

Characteristic: The berries have an acrid, bitter taste.

Parts used: The berries; sometimes the bark.

Applications:

Aerosol: Small quantities of Juniper may be burned like incense in hospital rooms or where sick patients reside in order to fumigate the air.

Antiseptic agent: Certain medical doctors in the 18th and 19th centuries often used Juniper oil in place of the well-known carbolic acid, to disinfect catgut, silk and surgical instruments.

Appetite: 2 ounces of gin prior to a meal. Juniper berries are used in the manufacture of gin.

Coughs and colds: A tea made of the berries and leaves; or the berries may be chewed slowly.

Diabetes: 4 capsules per day or 1 cup tea. More may be taken as needed.

Edema (fluid retention): Tea.

Epidemics: 6–8 capsules or 2–3 cups tea per day.

Epileptic fits: Rub spine, neck and chest with the oil.

Fevers: A tea combined with Wormwood.

Hairwash: The Indians living in the Maritime Provinces of Canada use the berries in decoction for greasy, oily scalp, dandruff and similar hair problems.

Heart stimulant: Capsules or tea.

Hives: Wash skin with Juniper tea.

Indigestion: Tea or capsules.

Kidney stones: Tea.

Leucorrhea: Vaginal douche with tea.

Liver (heart, kidney) stimulant: Tea.

Loose teeth: Juniper root dug from beneath the tree, cleaned and mashed in pulp form, then applied to the gums, will draw them closer around loose teeth, thereby strengthening them.

Lung congestion: Warm tea.

Pain in the abdomen or groin (abdominal cramps): Rub affected part with oil of Juniper.

Perspiration (to promote): Warm tea.

Placenta (to discharge): A brew made of the berries in some wine.

Rheumatism—arthritis: Reduce a decoction of the berries to the consistency of an extract and apply externally.

Sore throat (laryngitis): Gargle with warm tea.

Urination (to increase): Warm tea.

Venereal disease: Vaginal douche with strong decoction of berries.

Wounds: Wash with strong decoction of berries.

Kelp (Pelagophycus porra; Macrocystis pyrifera; Fucus versiculosus)
    Characteristic: Slightly saline and seaweed-tasting.
    Part used: Entire plant.

Note: Kelp is one member of a family of important seaweeds recognized for their medicinal value by doctors and scientists around the world. Other seaweeds used for such purposes are Irish moss, Iceland moss and various kinds of algae.

In this category for Kelp, therefore, we can also consider the other above-mentioned seaweeds, since they all possess certain identical constituents vital to medical science and food technology. Thus, when various purposes for use are listed below, they refer not only to Kelp specifically, but also the other seaweeds in general.

Applications:

Anemia: Capsules or use powdered herb as a food condiment.

Antibiotic (infection): The seaweeds have been found to produce strong antibiotic substances. Japanese scientists discovered that several species of Kelp and algae inhibit the growth of bacteria. It may be used safely wherever Goldenseal or powdered Garlic might be employed, but mostly for minor antibacterial use rather than major.

Bleeding (internal and external): Among most herbalists, Cayenne pepper, or Capsicum, is considered to be the ideal agent to stop bleeding. But now medical science has demonstrated the superior value of Kelp and related seaweeds. The alginic acid from Kelp has been used extensively in surgery to stop bleeding from venous sinuses, bone and extradural veins. A special kind of Kelp or alginic "wool" has been used in numerous hospitals, due to its highly absorbent and coagulant properties. The high sodium content in Kelp is one factor responsible for stopping hemorrhaging so quickly. Marine biologists have also observed that when such plants are injured, the alginic acid in their juices is exuded to react with the calcium in the sea water, which then becomes insoluble and forms a seal around the wound. It is a well-known fact that dried alginic acid absorbs 200–300 times its weight in water. For this reason it is widely used by food technologists as a conditioner in puddings, ice cream and pastries.

Kelp has also been recognized clinically for reducing internal inflammations as well.

Bleeding gums (grinding teeth): Massage infected, swollen and bleeding gums with a small mixture of powdered calcium and Kelp. The calcium will help the Kelp to coagulate the blood much better.

Chickenpox: Capsules or added to soup or broth.

Diarrhea: 3 capsules Kelp with 2 capsules cornstarch (internal).

Emaciation: Capsules, broth, or seasoning on food.

Gangrene: Powdered herb mixed with some Myrrh, made into a salve and rubbed on skin.

Gastroenteritis: Capsules or broth.

Hay fever: Capsules.

Indigestion: Capsules or seasoning for food, with a meal.

Intense fevers (malaria; typhoid): In the 19th century, arsenic was judiciously used for these conditions, for certain skin diseases, as well as anemia. But in this century it is no longer used. In Oriental countries like Japan and China, Kelp is used in place of arsenic for such types of fevers, in the forms of arsenate and arsenite, which are natural arsenic compounds available in trace amounts and contrary to popular thinking, are *not* toxic but of definite value.

Intestinal worms (roundworms; threadworms; nematodes): The kainic acid found in Kelp is strongly anthelmintic. It is a good idea to take some powdered Kelp with you when you travel to foreign countries, such as Mexico or China, where the water may present certain health hazards. Mix about ½ teaspoon of Kelp to 6–8 ounces of water before drinking. This will help to keep such worms out of intestines.

Lead and mercury poisoning (smog; carbon monoxide poisoning): Kelp is the best chelating agent for this purpose. Other agents include Garlic, Echinacea, Onion and Slippery Elm.

Measles, Mumps: See under chickenpox.

Obesity: The American herbalist Jethro Kloss said Kelp is "the best remedy for obesity."

Oral surgery (tooth extraction): Powdered Kelp, especially the extracted alginic acid, has been used by dentists upon their patients who have had tooth extractions or minor oral surgery.

Radiation poisoning: Because of seaweed and algae's strong absorbent qualities, large amounts of radiation can be removed from places of unwanted concentration. Additionally, Kelp can effectively remove radioactive strontium 90 from the body, according to one leading nutritionist.

Saliva: Food seasoning.

Scar tissue: Seaweeds, including Kelp, are useful for the prevention and elimination of pathological scar tissue. Carrageenan, a colloid substance extracted from seaweeds, especially the dark, purple kind like Irish moss, has been found to act as a stimulus for the production of collagenous granulation tissue in the body. Furthermore, when sufficient amounts of ascorbic acid or vitamin C are added to the diet as well, the collagenous tissue forms even more rapidly. Thus, vitamin C is a necessary adjunct to use with Kelp and related seaweeds. Now, the Kelp may be taken internally in capsules; but for the best results, a broth made of Kelp or a green drink is mixed in the blender with vitamin C added.

Ulcer: Capsules.

Weakness: Capsules; food seasoning; broth.

Non-medical uses:

Kelp makes an excellent organic fertilizer. Mix 1 part fish emulsion, 2 parts Kelp (powdered), 10 parts dried cow manure and 50 parts water. Mix in a closed container, then cover and let brew stand for several days, stirring occasionally to blend the ingredients together. Tomatoes, corn, squash, melons, peppers, and most flowering herbs and shrubs should respond to about 1 pint of this potion. Just pour half of it over the leaves and the rest around the base of the plant. Follow with a heavy watering. Kelp holds wonderful potential as a possible plant fuel or energy alternative for the immediate future. Marine scientists with the help of Navy frogmen have been transplanting large sections of Kelp on the ocean bottom in a special kind of "seaweed farm." Such wet plant biomass is a good source for liquid fuel (ethanol) and also to generate methane gas (a replacement for natural gas).

Lemon Balm (Melissa officinalis)

Characteristic: When fresh herb is crushed, it emits a strong lemon fragrance; hence the name.

Parts used: Herb, leaves.

Applications:

Dizziness (fainting spells): Infusion.

Drug addiction: Tea.

Emphysema: Tea.

Gallbladder: Tea.

Headache (migraine): Infusion.

Infection: Tea.

Insomnia: The fresh leaves inside pillow.

Leucorrhea: Vaginal douche with tea.

Liver (kidney; bladder stimulant): Warm tea with or without meals.

Memory stimulant (forgetfulness): Infusion, twice per day.

Monopause: Tea.

Menstruation (to promote): As a tea.

Nervousness (emotional disturbances): Infusion; 3–4 times per day.

Perspiration (to promote): Warm tea.

Smoking: Tea or capsules.

Sore throat: Gargle with tea.

Sores (bruises; bumps): Poultice of the crushed leaves.

Surgical dressing: Oil of Lemon Balm contains considerable ozone, of use in treating open wounds, cuts and bites.

Toothache: Crushed, fresh leaves applied to tooth.

Ulcer: Tea.

Urinary problems: Tea.

Non-medical uses:

To attract bees. If hives are rubbed with this herb, or it is planted near them, it will keep the bees always within close range, especially during swarming.

Lovage (Legusticum scoticum)

Characteristic: Strong odor and warm, aromatic flavor, similar to Celery.

Parts used: Root, leaves, seeds, young stems.

Applications:

Blood purifier: Tea.

Boils (pimples): Fresh leaves crushed and fried in a little olive oil, then applied directly will cause eruption and subsequent discharge of purulent matter.

Cancer: Tea.

Conjunctivitis: Strong decoction to drop into the eyes; or as wash for runny matter.

Cystitis (bladder inflammation; gallstones): Two teaspoons dried root in 1½ cups water. Bring to a boil; remove and let stand for 15 minutes. One cup three times daily.

Fainting spells: Tea.

Fevers: Warm tea.

Indigestion (heartburn): Warm tea.

Inflammation: Tea.

Intestinal mucus: Enema with strong decoction of herb.

Liver stimulant: Warm tea.

Lung congestion (asthma; bronchitis): An infusion of the root.

Memory: Tea.

Mild coughs: An infusion.

Obesity: Exerts an unknown influence.

Perspiration (to promote): Warm tea.

Pleurisy: A decoction, 4–5 times per day.

Rash: Skin wash made from tea.

Sexual desire: Tea.

Sore eyes (red eyes): An infusion made into an eyewash.

Sore throat: Gargle with warm tea.

Tetanus: 2 cups strong tea. And hot and cold packs soaked in two solutions of tea and applied externally.

Urination (to promote): Warm tea.

Mace (Myristica fragrans; Arillus myristicae; Myristica officinalis; Myristica mochata)

Characteristic: Strong Nutmeg flavor and smell.

Part used: The dried pulp of the Nutmeg kernel.

Applications:

Atherosclerosis: Tea (only exerts mild effect; Ginger root or Garlic works much better for this).

Bad breath: Mouthwash with tea.

Circulation (to improve): Warm tea, with Capsicum.

Diarrhea: Mix Mace and Nutmeg as a tea.

Fevers: Administer Mace tea, or Mace in some beverage.

Hypothermia (loss of body heat; physical refrigeration): Mace, Nutmeg, Cinnamon and Ginger will all stimulate production of body heat for the very young and the elderly. Use any of these four in warm milk or an agreeable fruit juice.

Oral hygiene: Put a little dab of powder on wet toothbrush and use in place of regular toothpaste. Do this occasionally or whenever needed.

Marjoram, Wild Oregano (Origanum vulgare)

Marjoram, Sweet Marjoram (Origanum majorana)

Characteristics: Acrid, pungent; strong Sage-like odor; reminiscent of Thyme.

Parts used: Marjoram)   *Sweet Marjoram)*
        Herb, oil   Herb, leaves
       Oregano)   *Marjoram)*

Applications:

Appetite: Season food with it to give it more appeal and aroma.

Bronchitis: Tea.

Cholesterol: Use with food as a seasoning. Also take capsules (2 per day) internally.

Epilepsy (fits, hysteria; seizures): Oil of Oregano applied warm on neck, spine, throat, chest.

Female abdominal cramps: Warm infusion until relieved.

Gout: Tea.

Indigestion (gastroenteritis): Warm tea.

Infectious childhood diseases: Warm infusion for measles, mumps, chickenpox and colic.

Insomnia: 2 capsules before retiring or 1 cup warm tea.

Menstruation (to regulate): Take tea 3–4 days in advance of period.

Minor headaches: Warm tea, and/or cool poultice on neck and head.

Motion sickness: Car, air and sea sickness; tea is made from the flowers of Marjoram.

Narcotics antidote (drug addiction): Strong infusion taken frequently.

Nervous shakes (Parkinson's disease; hand, limb trembling; physical tremors): A strong infusion of the herb and flowers; one cup, three to four times per day.

Rheumatism: Tea and/or warm packs on stiff joints.

Sexual desire: Tea made from the *fresh* plant only. Will not work as well if dried herb is used.

Toothache: Cotton soaked in oil and placed on cavity.

Whooping cough: Warm tea.

Sweet Marjoram, Marjoram

Applications:

Asthma: Warm tea twice per day.

Indigestion (stomach spasms): Warm tea of the leaves and flowers. Such a folk remedy is widely employed throughout much of the world. A recent scientific study of its use in Morocco for stomach problems verified clinically that the thymol and carvacrol in Marjoram block the release of calcium, thereby inhibiting spasms.

Infant colic: Warm tea.

Varicose veins (gout; rheumatism; arthritis): Warm tea internally; oil externally on calves and thighs.

Mustard, Black (Brassica nigra; Sinapis nigra)
Mustard, White (Brassica alba; Sinapis alba)

    Characteristics: Black mustard: Strongly pungent.
                White mustard: Mildly pungent.

    Part used: Black Mustard: The seeds.
           White mustard: The seeds.

    Applications:

    Black mustard:

    Backache: Mustard poultice for an hour. NOTE: Mustard should not make direct contact with skin. Have thin cloth material between it and skin.

    Indigestion: Promotes production of hydrochloric acid if taken in small amounts.

    Neuralgia: See backache.

    Paralysis: Rub limbs, joints in morning with strong wine. Apply Mustard poultices throughout the day. Massage in evening with olive oil very vigorously.

    Respiratory diseases (breathing difficulties; pneumonia): Strong tea; warm.

    Sciatica: See backache.

    White mustard:

    Antiseptic: Uses similar to those of Black Mustard.

    Appetite: As a food condiment.

    Bachache: Rub back with solution of White Mustard (powdered) mixed with some wine for relief. Solution should be warm for maximum effectiveness.

    Chronic bronchitis (lung congestion; pneumonia): Strong tea of the seeds.

    Constipation: Warm tea made of seeds.

    Indigestion: Warm tea.

    Pleurisy: Strong tea.

    Rheumatism (mild arthritis): Tea internally; poultice externally, especially on joints.

    Sore throat (strep throat; tonsillitis): Strong infusion as a gargle.

Nutmeg (Myristica fragrans; Myristica officinalis)
  Characteristic: Sweet spiciness and pleasant taste.
  Part used: The dried kernel of the seed.
  Applications:
    See listing for Mace.

Onion (Allium cepa)
  Characteristic: Distinctive odor due to the sulphur-containing volatile oil.
  Parts used: The root bulb, and occasionally the seeds.
  Applications:
    Antiseptic for reproductive organs: Onion exerts a strong antibacterial and hormone-like influence on both male and female systems. Has been used for venereal disease in some countries, like Mexico and Costa Rica.

    Atherosclerosis: Use raw to season food with; use frequently. NOTE: Onion salt (and Garlic salt) will *NOT* work for this. These only aggravate high blood pressure.

    Breathing difficulties: Warm Onion tea; a cut Onion held beneath nostrils and briefly inhaled.

    Bronchitis: Warm Onion tea or plain broth or soup with Onion added, taken internally.

    Burns (first, second, third degree): In the 16th century, medieval surgeons in England used Onion juice and olive or linseed oil to treat those suffering from gunpowder burnings, gunshot, sword, halbard, pike, lance, or other such wounds.

    Some Russian scientists in World War II used a paste made of macerated Onions on severe burns incurred by soldiers injured by mines and flame-throwers. These serious wounds did not become infected once the paste had been applied; and more rapid healing ensued with those upon whom the Onion paste had been diligently used.

    Coughs: See bronchitis.

    Diabetes: Use frequently to season food. Onion broth or soup each day, too.

    Gallbladder: An Onion or Garlic enema will stimulate gallbladder.

    Hemorrhoids: Thin slice of raw Onion inserted in rectum to reduce inflammation, and relieve itching.

Hives: An Onion salve applied to skin for relief.

Hoarseness: Gargle with warm Onion tea or clear soup or broth for relief.

Hypertension: Use frequently to season food.

Intestinal purifier: An Onion tea enema.

Lead and mercury poisoning: Frequent use as a food spice and Onion broth or soup often.

Liver stimulant: Onion broth or soup; Onion tea enema.

Sinusitis: See under breathing difficulties.

Ulcer (external): Poultice of raw Onion slice to site of infection.

Ulcer (internal): Onion broth.

Venomous bites: See ulcer (external).

Warts: See ulcer (external).

Wounds: See ulcer (external).

Oregano: See Marjoram

Paprika, Hungarian Paprika (Capsicum annuum)
  Characteristic: Sometimes tasteless, sometimes pungent and slightly sweet as a Capsicum, depending on the species.
  Part used: Ripe and dried fruit.
  Applications:
    Canker sores: One half teaspoon in warm water; gargle, rinse mouth; same may be taken internally as well.
    Common cold: Paprika in hot chicken soup.
    Infant colic (intestinal gas): Mild tea or in food.
    Intestinal gas: Food condiment or tea.
    Kidney infection: Use in broth or juice.
    Scurvy (rickets): Broth, juice, and in food.

Parsley (Petroselinum crispum; Petroselinum sativum)
  Characteristic: Sweet, mildly spicy and refreshing.
  Parts used: Herb, leaves, root and seeds.
  Applications:
    Breast milk (to diminish): Crushed leaves, moistened with Camphor and applied to the breasts, will help dry up the milk of mothers.
    Cancer: Use generously in green drink or with other herbs like Garlic, Comfrey and carrots. Works best in fresh form. An enema of Parsley-peach bark or leaf tea is of

use in stimulating the liver, to help it throw off excess toxins. Has high histidine content, which inhibits further growth of most cancer cells.

Coughs: Six ounce raw green juice sipped slowly.

External swellings: Poultice for swollen glands and breasts.

Eye infection: Wash eyes with cool Parsley tea on a daily basis.

Eyesight: See eye infection. Take Parsley (raw juice or capsules) internally each day.

Gallstones (to dissolve): Tea or green drink.

Gout: Raw juice or tea each day.

Hypertension: See gout.

Indigestion: Chew some fresh sprigs or take some raw juice or Parsley tea.

Kidney stones: Tea, green juice, soups, or eaten fresh.

Lice: An ointment made of the seeds and leaves.

Liver diseases (jaundice; hepatitis; cirrhosis): Tea, green juice, salads, soups, or by itself, consumed raw.

Menstruation: Parsley tea daily.

Scalp problems (dandruff; ringworm or tinea capitis): Make a tea of the crushed seeds and use as a hairwash frequently. May be combined with Black Walnut.

Semen discharge (nocturnal emission): A daily dose of 50–100 grams of Parsley juice taken internally.

Venomous bites: Eight ounce glass raw green juice (internal) and Parsley poultice (external).

Venereal disease: Eight ounce raw green juice daily and Parsley tea douche.

Peppermint (Mentha piperita)

Characteristic: Entire plant has a distinct aroma. A hot and aromatic sensation is experienced at first; but a coolness is felt immediately afterwards in the mouth.

Part used: Leaves.

Applications:

Arthritis (rheumatism; neuralgia): Apply oil on painful joints and swellings; use heat, too.

Electric shock: Tea (internal). Oil of Peppermint rubbed on vital areas of body (heart, abdomen, temples, neck, spine and bottom of feet) in a slow rotating massage. Peppermint poultices applied on neck, spine, chest, forehead, abdomen. Alternate between hot and cold poultices.

Fevers: Cool tea to reduce body temperature.

Gallbladder: Tea or enema for stimulation.

Heart trouble of any kind: Warm tea as tonic for cardiac disorders.

Hives: Wash skin with cool tea for relief of itching. Take tea internally to strengthen nerves.

Hypothermia: Hot tea (internally): hot Peppermint bath; rub numb areas with oil of Peppermint briskly.

Insanity (convulsions; hysteria): Warm tea and Peppermint oil on spine, neck, throat, temples and chest. Use Wood Betony and some Caraway in the tea.

Insomnia: Warm tea before retiring.

Liver stimulant (bile production): Warm tea with meals.

Migraine headaches: Warm tea and/or oil rubbed on temples.

Nervousness: Warm tea. Use an equal part of Wood Betony and some Caraway as well.

Smoking: Tea (internal) to relieve sore throat and stop hacking cough.

Stimulant: Jethro Kloss says the tea works more powerfully on the system than liquor does. He recommends it for loss of body heat, fainting, dizziness and in place of aspirin.

Stomach problems (gastroenteritis; heartburn): Warm tea with or without meals.

Tonsillitis: Gargle with *strong* decoction of the leaves frequently.

Pickling spice (a blend)

Characteristic: Pungent and spicy.

Herbs used: Allspice, Bay Leaves, Black Pepper, Cardamom, Chilies, Cinnamon, Cloves, Coriander, Ginger, Mace, Mustard.

Note: For the following health problems, use this preparation: One tablespoonful of Pickling spice to one pint boiling water. Let simmer on low heat for about five minutes. Remove. Cover. Steep for 25 minutes. Strain and use. Use only stainless steel, unchipped enamelware, or glassware.

Abdominal cramps

Common cold

Constipation

Hypothermia (loss of body heat)

Influenza

Intestinal gas

Poor circulation

Stimulant for sluggish liver, gallbladder

Pumpkin pie spice (a blend)

Characteristic: Pleasantly sweet and mildly spicy.

Herbs used: Cinnamon, Ginger, Nutmeg, Allspice.

Applications:

Adjuvant for purgatives: See Allspice.

Burns: Tea (Internal) for mild, calming effect.

Halitosis (bad breath): Use as a mouthwash in tea form.

Indigestion (gas): Warm tea.

Mild diabetes (or hypoglycemia): Warm tea for those who have borderline blood-sugar problems.

Mild insomnia: Make into a tea or use in warm milk; ½ teaspoon to six ounces milk.

Mild internal bleeding (minor ulcers): Warm tea.

Mild nervousness: Warm tea.

Ulcer (Internal): Warm tea.

Rosemary (Rosmarinus officinalis)

Characteristic: Refreshing; piny; resinous; pungent.

Parts used: Herb and root.

Applications:

Appetite: Use as a food condiment.

Bad breath (halitosis): Tea as a mouthwash.

Bronchitis (asthma): Tea or syrup prepared with equal parts Rosemary, Mullein and Coltsfoot.

Coughs: Warm tea.

Headaches: Tea.

Heart stimulant: Tea or capsules.

Intestinal gas (indigestion): Warm tea.

Liver tonic: Warm tea.

Low blood pressure: Warm tea or capsulated powders will help to elevate blood pressure.

Menopause: Tea or capsules.

Nervousness: Tea or capsules.

Poor circulation: Warm tea or food seasoned with Rosemary.

Rheumatism: Tea or hot/cold packs soaked in strong decoctions.

Scalp problems (premature baldness; scurf; dandruff): Decoction used as hairwash.

Urinary problems: Tea (internal).

Wounds (sores): Oil of Rosemary used externally.

Saffron (Crocus sativus)
Characteristic: Exhibits an exotic, but delicate, pleasantly bittersweet flavor.
Part used: The stigmas.
Applications:
Appetite stimulant: A little of the oil in various liquors.
Bronchitis: Warm tea.
Chronic uterine bleeding: Douche with tea.
Fevers: Alone as a tea or with Catnip.
Gout (varicose veins): Externally as a salve.
Heart stimulant: Warm tea.
Intestinal gas (indigestion): Warm tea.
Menstruation (to promote): Tea or douche.
Perspiration (to promote): Warm tea.
Varicose veins: Warm tea (internal); poultices (external).
Whooping cough: Warm tea internally and as a gargle.

Note: Not to be confused with Meadow Saffron (*Colchicum autumnale*), which is poisonous, or American Saffron (*Carthamus tinctorius*), also known as Safflower.

Sage, common garden (Salvia officinalis)
Characteristic: Pungent, warm, astringent.
Parts used: Leaves, the whole herb.
Applications:
Antibacterial agent: A wash with tea.
Common cold: Warm tea often.
Diarrhea: Cold tea or capsules.
Dizziness: Sip slowly some cold tea.
Fevers (typhoid; scarlet; malaria): Warm tea.
Gastroenteritis: Warm tea with meal.
Hair loss: Rinse scalp daily with decoction of Sage. Rub small amount of Sage oil into scalp and massage well each day.

Headache: Cool tea.

Indigestion: Warm tea.

Insect bites and stings: Freshly-bruised Sage on skin; or poultice made of Sage tea.

Intestinal gas: Warm tea.

Leucorrhea: Douche.

Lung congestion (bronchitis; hoarseness; influenza): Warm tea.

Menstruation: Warm tea (internal) and/or warm douche.

Nervous disorders (Parkinson's disease; trembling; shakes): Plenty of warm tea.

Night sweats (to stop them): Lukewarm tea as often as needed (internal).

Oral hygiene (canker sores; bleeding gums): Use tea as a mouthwash. Use powdered Sage on toothbrush for gums and teeth; rub some powder on canker sores.

Pain from measles and mumps: Warm tea to relieve muscle and joint pain.

Scabies: Wash skin with decoction of Sage.

Secretions (to reduce): Sage tea reduces saliva flow, excess perspiration, etc.

Sexual desire (excessive): Very warm tea.

Sore throat: Gargle with very warm tea to which has been added a little sea salt and lemon juice.

Spasms (cramps; fits): Sage tea for epilepsy, taken with regularity.

Tonsillitis (strep throat): Gargle with strong decoction.

Ulcer (external): Wash skin with decoction.

Ulcer (internal): Warm tea.

Warts: Sage poultice as often as needed.

Non-medical uses:

Insect repellent: Rub Sage oil on skin to keep mosquitoes and gnats away.

Natural insecticide: Strong solutions of Sage may be sprayed on garden vegetables to keep some unwanted pests away.

Savory, summer (Satureia hortensis)
Savory, winter (Satureia montana)

Characteristics: Warm, aromatic; resinous; delicate Sage flavor.

Note: Winter savory stronger than Summer savory.

Part used: The herb.

Applications:

Diarrhea: Tea.

Eyesight: Wash eyes daily with mild tea solution.

Fevers: Adds flavor to such bitter fever-herbs as Yarrow and Boneset.

Headache: Cool tea.

Influenza (common cold): Equal parts of Savory, Yarrow and Boneset as a tea.

Intestinal gas: Savory tea or chew some fresh herb.

Lung congestion (asthma; hoarseness; mucus accumulations): Strong tea, taken warm.

Nausea (vomiting): Tea.

Nervous disorders: Cool tea.

Saliva (to stimulate it): Warm tea or chew fresh herb.

Sexual desire: Warm tea.

Sore throat (laryngitis): Gargle with tea.

Stomach disorders (gastroenteritis; indigestion): Tea.

Toothache: Oil of Savory on wad of cotton and applied inside mouth on site of pain.

Weakness: Warm tea or clear broth/soup made with Savory in it.

Sesame (Sesamum indicum)

Characteristic: Toasted; nutlike flavor.

Part used: The seeds.

Applications:

Common cold (influenza): The seeds are rich in vitamins C and E, and in calcium. Grind some up into a fine powder and use in chicken soup or some warm broth during the flu season. Builds resistance to germs.

Lice: Seed oil externally.

Obesity: Reduces serum cholesterol in the bloodstream. Eat with meals.

Poor eyesight (dim vision; weak eyes): Grind some of the seeds and add them to a warm infusion of Eyebright. Let set a while until cool, then strain through a fine cheesecloth or muslin. Use clear liquid as an eyewash. The oil from the seeds will enhance the medicinal performance of Eyebright considerably, as well as afford a natural emollient for the eyes themselves.

Premature births (premature babies): German scientists experimented with Sesame seed oil on a clinical trial basis in the 1930s. They found that those babies born prematurely, who received around 20 drops of Sesame oil per day, gained weight and experienced an increase in hemoglobin, which enabled them to breathe a lot better—often without a respirator.

Scar tissue (recent): Rub oil of Sesame on recent incision to keep proud flesh from forming.

Spleen nutrient: Sesame seeds can benefit the spleen due to certain nutritional factors in them. Since the spleen is the organ responsible for filtering and storing blood in the body, it would be a good idea to incorporate the seeds into your diet regularly.

Staph infection: Use oil externally; eat the seeds.

Stress (unusually high tension): Sesame seeds may enable a person under a great deal of stress to cope better in such a tension-filled environment.

Weakness: Sesame seed butter or oil as food items to be consumed in meals. Warm Sesame seed tea internally. Grind up roasted seeds into coarse meal and sprinkle on top of other food.

Non-medical uses:

In the Near East where Sesame is common, the plant is often found growing near caves and crevices in the surrounding rocks. Historical tradition has suggested that on several occasions, the presence of Sesame plant by a cave often led to the discovery of remarkable treasures therein. One was connected with Ali Baba's famous line—"Open Sesame!"—when the entrance opened as if by magic to these words. The other, more reliable reference, had to do with an insignificant fifteen-year-old Bedouin boy in 1947, who chased after his runaway goat and finally found the animal contentedly chewing on some succulent Sesame plant in front of an open cave. Mohammed adh-Dhib entered and discovered a mélange of broken pottery and a number of dusty, old manuscript fragments scattered about. Thus was the hidden archaeological treasure of the Dead Sea Scrolls finally brought to light after many centuries and the rest of the story has now become history, all due to the uncanny spots near to which Sesame frequently chooses to grow.

Slippery Elm (Ulmus fulva)

Characteristic: This is one herb which has a unique taste all its own. It is not bitter, but rather mild and pleasant. However, the most distinguishing feature is its filmy, slick taste, but lacking any kind of oiliness whatsoever.

Parts used: Inner bark (often called the cambium); and, rarely, the root.

Applications:

When I was a boy of about eight years old, I came down with an acute case of appendicitis. My father, who had inherited a great deal of herbal knowledge from his mother, brewed up a batch of Slippery Elm tea for me to take. Within three days I was on my feet once again and off to school. From personal experience, I know it works and thus encourage fathers and mothers everywhere to rely upon this. If a child is taught early enough to monitor his or her own bowel movements, then such a condition may never come about.

Allergies: Tea or capsule frequently.

Blood clotting (to prevent it): Tea or capsule frequently.

Blood clotting (to promote it during hemorrhaging): Apply powdered bark externally to site of bleeding in loose form.

Burns (1st, 2nd, 3rd degree):Follow instructions under gangrene.

Cancer: Tea or broth to be given often each day for nourishment and to regain strength.

Colitis: Tea, broth or enema.

Constipation: Mix two teaspoons of powdered Elm bark with one ounce brown sugar or maple syrup; then add one-half pint warm milk and water, plus one ounce of olive oil. Stir and take.

Diarrhea: Administer as enema the following ingredients in infusion form: one teaspoon powdered Slippery Elm bark; three teaspoons powdered Bayberry bark; one teaspoon powdered Skullcap in one-half pint boiling water; remove, cover, let cool for one-half hour; strain, then add one teaspoon tincture Myrrh, and give lukewarm.

Eyesight (to improve and for inflammation): Bathe eyes frequently with cool tea.

Fevers (typhoid; malaria; scarlet; rocky mountain spotted): Strong tea of bark. One cup every 2 to 3 hours in the daytime; and one cup every four hours at night before retiring.

Gangrene (wounds; open sores; exposed flesh; abscesses): Make a paste as follows: Mix the powder with hot water to form the required consistency; spread smoothly upon soft cotton cloth and apply over the parts affected. If applied to hairy parts of the body, first spread olive oil on poultice to prevent paste sticking to skin.

Hemorrhaging: See under blood clotting (to promote it).

Hives: Tea (internal) and poultices (external).

Lead and mercury poisoning: Tea or capsules frequently.

Leucorrhea: Tea or capsules; douche.

Liver stimulant: Warm tea or enema.

Mucus accumulations (bronchitis): Strong tea, pinch of Cayenne pepper, and touch of Clover honey. Slippery Elm will bind up mucus inside the body and pass the unwanted residue out through the intestines. For any kind of lung congestion—i.e., asthma, bronchitis, etc.— take one-and-one-half teaspoons Flaxseed, and one-half ounce Cayenne pepper, two ounces Slippery Elm bark, one stick of Cinnamon, a few Cloves, and some Licorice root. Add everything to one-and-one-quarter quarts water. Simmer on low heat for about half an hour. Strain and add one pint apple cider vinegar and one pint Clover honey or pure maple syrup. Allow to cool; then bottle with stopper or cork. Two tablespoons every 3 to 4 hours.

Pregnancy: Tea or capsules daily throughout entire nine month period for nourishment.

Premature birth (to prevent it): See pregnancy.

Scar tissue: Tea or capsules (internal); poultices (external). Will only work for recent surgery, incisions, etc. to prevent it from occurring. Won't work too well for getting rid of old scar tissue.

Scurvy: Tea or broth frequently.

Skin discoloration: Poultice.

Smoking: Tea to relieve sore throat; stop hacking cough.

Sore throat: See smoking.

Tonsillitis: Warm tea.

Toothache (cavity): A pinch of powder in the cavity or on the site of pain.

Tuberculosis: Warm tea.

Venereal disease: Tea or capsules frequently (internal consumption). Also douche.

Weakness (emaciation; food for the sick; recovery from major illness): Slippery Elm tea or food is one of the best things to administer. To make the food, mix one teaspoon powder with cold water and then pour on one pint boiling water, stirring constantly. Flavor with Cinnamon, Nutmeg, Mace or Citrus rind if so desired. This thin, smooth paste makes an excellent substance to eat. Slippery Elm is one of the *most nutritious* herbs in nature! Another method of food preparation is to beat one egg with one teaspoon powdered bark, adding some boiling milk over it, with a little honey added for flavor.

Whooping cough: Strong tea flavored with a little Clover honey and pinch of lemon.

Worms: Powdered Elm bark and ground pumpkin seeds in pineapple juice.

Spearmint (Mentha viridis; Mentha spicata; Mentha crispus; Mentha cardiaca)

Characteristic: Slightly pungent and aromatic, but lacking the cool sensation experienced when chewing fresh leaves as found with Peppermint.

Part used: The herb.

Applications:

Abdominal cramps (stomach spasms): 2 to 5 drops of Spearmint oil or several cups of tea.

Chickenpox: Warm tea. Also administer tea well in advance of epidemic to keep your child from getting it or measles or mumps.

Earache: Combine equal portions of Spearmint and Mullein oil. Apply a few drops of warm oil in ears.

Fevers: Warm tea.

Hemorrhoids (piles): Apply tincture locally.

Hiccoughs: A few drops of oil of Spearmint on the back of the throat.

Indigestion (intestinal gas; infant colic): Warm tea with or without meals.

Inflammation: Warm tea.

Kidney stones: Tincture of Spearmint.

Measles—mumps: See chickenpox.

Nausea (vomiting): Warm tea, or a few drops of the plant oil.

Nervousness: Tea.

Rheumatism: Rub the joints with oil of Spearmint, then apply heat pad.

Scalding urine (lack of urination): Tea.

Sunflower (Helianthus annuus)

Characteristic: Nut-like, slightly oily and somewhat sweet taste.

Parts used: The seeds; sometimes the flowers and leaves; the root rarely.

Applications:

Arthritis (rheumatism): Take the entire head of the Sunflower plant when the seeds begin to ripen and cut it into small pieces. Place in a stone or earthenware vessel with some soap chips and vodka. Soak in the sun for about ten days. Use the aged liniment on painful, swollen joints.

Burns (sunburn): Salve made of the crushed root pulp and the seed oil.

Cancer: Grind up seeds into coarse meal; add to food for more nourishment. Also take oil internally.

Cholesterol (to reduce): Sunflower seed oil is high in linoleate and lecithin which are known factors in reducing serum cholesterol in the blood and preventing atherosclerosis.

Fevers (malaria; typhoid; scarlet; rheumatic): Decoction of flowers and leaves.

Gallbladder stimulant: Infusion of one teaspoon oil daily.

Hepatitis (jaundice; cirrhosis of the liver): Strong decoction of the seeds.

Inflammation of gallbladder and kidney: Decoction of flowers and leaves.

Lung congestion (asthma; pneumonia; common cold; whooping cough): Make the following preparation: Boil three ounces of seeds in one quart of water; reduce to 15 ounces and strain. Add 4 to 5 ounces of good brandy and one-half to one ounce of rum and five ounces of honey. Mix well. Store in cool, dry place. Give in doses of one tablespoon for adults and one teaspoon for children, 4 to 5 times per day for any of the above complaints.

Scar tissue (to prevent it): Oil (internal or external). Only good for recent surgery, etc. Won't work very well on old scar tissue already formed.

Skin cancer: Extract of the fresh flowers.

Smoking habit: An M.D. at the Sunset Kaiser-Permanente Medical Center in California counsels his patients who wish to quit the smoking habit, to chew raw, shelled Sunflower seeds, which seems to satisfy the craving for tobacco.

Snakebites (scorpion stings; insect bites and stings): The crushed root is applied as a wet poultice.

Weakness: See cancer.

Whooping cough: Tea made of ground seeds.

Tarragon (Artemisia dracunculus)

Characteristic: Licorice-Anise flavor; pleasant, slightly bitter.

Parts used: Dried leaves and flowering tops.

Applications:

Appetite (to improve): Tea to stimulate.

Bad breath (halitosis): Tea as a gargle and mouthwash.

Flavoring agent for bitter herbs: Makes herbs like Valerian, Goldenseal and Chaparral more palatable.

Insomnia: Warm tea.

Menstruation (to promote): Tea.

Rabies (Hydrophobia): Strong decoction on an empty stomach.

Urination (to promote): Tea.

Venomous poisons: The freshly-crushed herb applied externally helps to draw out toxins from rattlesnake bites, spider bites, scorpion, hornet, wasp and bee stings.

Worms: Warm tea (internal).

Thyme (Thymus vulgaris)

Characteristics: Strong; pleasant; pungent Clove flavor.

Part used: The herb.

Applications:

Alcoholism: Warm tea to stimulate liver.

Blood-cleanser: Equal parts of Thyme leaves, Echinacea rootstock, Yellow dock root and Sarsaparilla rootstock in two pints water. Boil five minutes. Add Thyme flowers. Steep one-half hour. Drink three cups daily.

Bubonic plague: Strong tea (internal); aerosol spray made from strong decoction; burn Thyme herb in sick room as incense in order to sterilize air; give patient a Thyme bath.

Burns: Soak gauze in decoction of Thyme prior to applying to burns.

Cirrhosis of liver: See alcoholism.

Diabetes: Tea.

Female problems (infections in uterus, vagina, etc.): Douche made from strong decoction of herb.

Fevers (scarlet; malaria; etc.): Strong tea as drink.

Gangrene: Thyme has been used clinically in Europe as a substitute for carbolic acid and oil of turpentine. Its strong antiseptic qualities make it a superb wash for gangrenous flesh.

Hysterics: Warm tea.

Infections (general): Strong tea for internal-external uses.

Insect repellent: Equal parts of Thyme, Marjoram, Pennyroyal and Lavender in an ointment or liquid lotion to repel insects.

Insomnia: Cool tea.

Intestinal purifier: Strong tea or enema.

Leprosy: Wash skin with strong tea.

Lung congestion (bronchitis; emphysema; influenza): Strong tea to drink; also inhale vapors.

Rheumatism (arthritis; neuralgia; bursitis): Oil of Thyme rubbed on painful joints.

Skin disorders (discoloration; eczema; psoriasis; poison ivy rash; ringworm): Use the tincture or strong decoction externally as a wash frequently.

Sores: See leprosy.

Tetanus: Strong tea (internal) and hot/cold packs soaked in Thyme tea (external).

Toothache: Cotton soaked with oil of Thyme and applied on site of pain.

Throat problems (strep throat; laryngitis): Strong tea as

drink; also the vapors of the hot tea as an inhalant. Oil
of Thyme on a handkerchief and inhaled is also useful.

Tuberculosis: Warm tea frequently.

Vaginitis: See female problems.

Varicose veins (gout): Oil of Thyme rubbed on afflicted
limbs; cover with flannel.

Venereal disease: See female problems.

Whooping cough (common cold; influenza): Thyme syrup.
Make tea of one ounce dried leaves to one pint boiling
water. Cool. Strain. Add one cup pure Clover honey.
Stir until mixed. Refrigerate. Take tablespoon doses at
least seven times per day.

Worms (intestinal parasites): Tea or powdered capsule.

Turmeric (Curcuma longa)

Characteristic: Aromatic; pepper-like; acrid; mildly warm;
woody-spicy aroma.

Part used: The underground rhizome.

Applications:

Blood impurities: A tea. Or, the powdered spice in capsule. One or two capsules, three times daily.

Cholesterol: The dimethylbenzyl alcohol in Turmeric reduces serum cholesterol in blood. The curcumin or yellow coloring factor counteracts accumulations of ingested
cholesterol in the liver.

Coughs (common cold): Tea.

Electric Shock: Warm tea (internal). Use in conjunction
with Black Mustard, Cayenne Pepper, etc. to revive.

Eye discharge (conjunctivitis; opthalmia): The powder made
into an eyewash.

Gout: Tea (internal) and poultice (external) for relief.

Indigestion: Turmeric increases mucin content of stomach
gastric juices so as to reduce the irritation of pungent
spices like Chili Peppers.

Inflammation: See gout.

Intestinal parasites (worms): Tea or capsules.

Liver stimulant: Enhances value of Dandelion, when the
two are used together.

Rheumatoid arthritis (joint inflammation; gout; varicose
veins): Turmeric is similar to hydrocortisone in its anti-
inflammatory activity.

Staph infection: Its outstanding antioxidant properties kill staph germs rather well. Turmeric is a safe spice with no side effects whatsoever.

Varicose veins: See gout.

Note: The curcumin (yellow-coloring agent) in Turmeric has a molecular structure very similar to that of NDGA (nordihydroguaiaretic acid) in Chaparral (Larrea species).

Non-medical uses:

A preservative to extend the shelf-life of oils and fats. Turmeric has replaced synthetic yellow coat-tar colors in orangeades and lemonades made in Europe.

Watercress (Nasturtium officinale)

Characteristic: Yields a pleasing, peppery taste.

Part used: The herb.

Applications:

Anemia: Raw, green juice drink once a day.

Asthma: See anemia. Watercress tea to expel mucus.

Atherosclerosis: See anemia.

Blood purifier: The Pennsylvania Germans would employ Watercress as one of their many blutreinigungsmittel for purifying the blood every Spring.

Cancer: Drink raw, green juice at least twice a day. Watercress is high in histidine, which clinically has been found to inhibit the multiplication of certain cancer viruses.

Eczema (psoriasis): Make an infusion of cress this way: wash a large handful and put into a clean saucepan. Add enough cold water to cover, bring to a boil and simmer slowly until quite tender. Strain through muslin or cheesecloth and allow to cool. Bathe the afflicted skin with this freely. Also good for roughness of the skin caused by frequent exposure to the weather. Farmers, seamen and others will especially benefit from this.

Gout: Green drink daily or tea.

Headaches: A handful of Watercress, having been well-washed, should be put into a jug and a pint of boiling apple cider vinegar added. Allow to cool, then stir well, strain and bottle for use. When the headache occurs, wet a handkerchief with the vinegar and lay it on the brow.

Hives: Green drink daily or tea (internal).

Kidney stones: See hives. Or use tea generously to break them up and expel them from system.

Oral hygiene: Rinse mouth each morning with strong tea for a clean, lively feeling. Or chew sprigs of fresh herb.

Scurvy: Watercress has enough vitamin C or ascorbic acid to correct this deficiency.

Weakness: Use fresh herb on salads, soups, green drink, or tea for strength and vitality.

White Pepper (Piper album)

Characteristic: Less aromatic than Black Pepper but with a more delicate flavor.

Part used: From the same plant (*P. nigrum*) as Black Pepper, but is the dried fruit with the outer part of the pericarp removed by soaking in water, followed by rubbing and then drying.

Applications:

Constipation: One teaspoon in warm water twice a day to correct obstinate constipation in those with poor digestions.

Fevers (malaria and cholera): Warm tea given often.

Stomachache: Used in the People's Republic of China in tea form to correct this as well as abdominal pains.

SECTION TWO

Culinary Uses

This section contains listings of each of the herbs and spices introduced in the first section, arranged according to the many ways in which they may be used in ordinary food preparation. In addition, there are several informative essays on beer and alcoholic beverages, use of oils, reducing sodium intake and sprouting.

PART ONE
Culinary Uses by Food Category

Beans:	Black Pepper; Capsicum; Caraway; Cloves; Coriander; Ginger (reduces gas); Kelp; Onion; Paprika; Pumpkin Pie Spice (with Boston Baked); Sage (lima beans); Savory; Sesame seed; Spearmint (bean and soup purees); Tarragon; Turmeric; Watercress (with bean sprouts).
Beer:	Borage; Cumin; Juniper; Marjoram; Kelp (kelceloid holds beer foam).
Beverages: (Coffee substitutes)	Burdock root (coffee substitute); Dandelion root (use with Chicory root); Sunflower seeds (roasted or fried). Other plants used as beverages in various parts of the world include: Chicory roots (southern United States); Senna seeds (Central and South America); fruit of Spanish Chestnut (Mediterranean countries); seeds and root of Chick Pea (Europe and Asia); Asparagus, Carob seeds (Middle East); Hawthorn seeds (British Isles); Carrot root, Yam root (Mexico); Bedstraw fruit, Soybean seed and Mountain Ash fruit (Kentucky, Tennessee and the Ozarks).
Beverages: (General, cider, tea, lemonade)	Borage (tea); Crab Apple (herbal root beer); Cinnamon (with hot apple cider); Ginger; Lemon Balm (breakfast tea); Mace; Coriander (lemonade); Nutmeg; Peppermint; Spearmint (teas and punch); Turmeric (natural coloring

substitute, used in Europe as replacement for coal-tar derivative agents in orangeade and lemonade).

Breadstuffs: Anise; Caraway; Cardamom; Coriander; Fen-
(Breads, biscuits,   nel; Garlic; Dandelion flowers (in cheese muf-
dinner rolls)   fins); Onion; Rosemary; Saffron; Sesame
                          seeds; Tarragon in pumpernickel and dark
                          rye; Sunflower seeds (with nut breads).

Breakfast Entrees: Basil; Black pepper; Capsicum; Caraway;
(Eggs)   Chives; Cumin; Fennel; Garlic; Kelp; Oregano;
                          Marjoram (soufflés); Mustard, Onion; Parsley;
                          Rosemary; Saffron; Savory (soufflés); Sesame
                          seeds; Thyme; Turmeric; Watercress.

Breakfast Entrees: Cardamom (makes phytic acid in grains more
(Grain cereals)   digestible); Cinnamon; Mace; Nutmeg; Pump-
                          kin Pie Spice; Savory; Slippery Elm (with
                          bran).

Breakfast Entrees: Cinnamon; Crab Apple (used diced in batter,
(Pancakes,   especially sourdough or buttermilk); Dande-
waffles)   lion flowers (in sourdough or buttermilk
                          batter); Mace; Nutmeg.

Cabbage Dishes: Allspice; Capsicum; Caraway; Cumin; Dill;
(Corn Beef,   Fennel; Kelp; Mustard; Parsley; Pickling Spice;
sauerkraut)   Savory; Spearmint (used in Wales with boiled
                          cabbage); Tarragon.

Casseroles: Basil; Bay; Black and White Pepper; Capsi-
                          cum; Celery seeds; Chives; Garlic; Kelp;
                          Onion; Oregano; Marjoram; Parsley; Sesame
                          seeds; Turmeric (noodles, macaroni dishes).

Chinese Cuisine: Anise; Borage; Chinese Angelica (*Dong guei*
                          or *Tang kuei*); Black and White Pepper; Chives;
                          Caraway; Coriander (sweet-sour); Cumin;
                          Ginger; Kelp; Lovage (sautéed vegetable
                          dishes).

Dairy: (Cheeses)	Annatto (coloring); Basil; Caraway; Coriander: Cumin (soft cheeses); Celery seeds; Dandelion flowers (home-made cheddars); Horseradish (with gorgonzola and bleu cheeses); Mace; Marjoram (cream cheese); Onion; Saffron (coloring); Sage; Thyme; Watercress (cream cheese).
Dairy: (Cottage Cheese)	Anise: Capsicum; Caraway; Chives; Dandelion; Dill; Kelp; Marjoram; Onion; Paprika; Parsley; Sage; Sesame seeds; Thyme; White Pepper.
Dairy: (Dips, sour cream)	Capsicum; Caraway; Chives; Cumin; Dill; Garlic; Kelp; Lovage; Marjoram; Mustard; Oregano; Paprika; Parsley; Watercress.
Dairy: (Milk and butter)	Annatto (coloring); Cinnamon (hot milk upon retiring or in the winter); Saffron (coloring); Sage (with hot milk after skating in the winter—a custom in Holland); Tarragon (butter); Turmeric (butter).
Desserts: (Candies)	Angelica; Anise; Borage; Caraway; Coriander; Cumin; Fennel; Peppermint; Pumpkin Pie Spice; Sesame; Thyme; Tarragon.
Desserts: (Custards and puddings)	Angelica (stem); Bay (leaf); Cardamom; Cinnamon; Ginger; Mace; Nutmeg; Pumpkin Pie Spice; Sunflower seeds.
Desserts: (Cakes, cookies)	Caraway; Cardamom; Cloves; Coriander; Fennel; Ginger; Mace; Saffron; Sesame seeds; Spearmint.
Desserts: (Ice cream)	(Flavorings): Allspice; Angelica; Cardamom; Cinnamon; Ginger; Mace; Nutmeg; Pumpkin Pie Spice; Peppermint; Spearmint (colorings): Annatto; Saffron; Tarragon; Turmeric.

Desserts: Anise; Cardamom; Cinnamon; Coriander;
(Pastries)   Mace; Nutmeg; Fennel; Saffron.

Desserts: Anise; Caraway; Cumin; Cinnamon; Ginger;
(Pies and pie   Mace, Cardamom; Nutmeg.
filling)

Far East Cuisine: Angelica with curry dishes; Caraway; Cumin;
(Egyptian,   Curry powder: Coriander, Anise, Garlic, Mus-
Indian, Persian)   tard (for Hindu dishes like chutney); Ginger;
                     Kelp; Parsley; Peppermint (used fresh in
                     tossed salads in Israel); Saffron (curry); Tur-
                     meric (curry).

Fruits: Allspice (baked apples, pears); Angelica (stem
(Baked, cooked)   used); Anise (use sparingly in fruit stews);
                     Basil (compotes); Coriander; Crab Apple
                     (baked apples); Cardamom; Fennel (baked
                     apples, pears); Ginger; Lemon Balm (citrus
                     fruits); Mace; Nutmeg; Peppermint; Rosemary;
                     Sesame seeds (fruit salads); Turmeric (citrus
                     fruit).

German Cuisine: Garlic; Horseradish (with liverwurst); Kelp;
(see also cabbage,   Mustard; Onion; Paprika; Parsley; Pickling
various meats,   Spice (sauerbraten); Rosemary; Sesame;
and potatoes)   Tarragon.

Gravies: Bay, Black and White Pepper (chicken gravies,
                     etc.); Capsicum; Celery seed; Fennel; Garlic;
                     Horseradish (for sauerbraten gravy); Kelp;
                     Onion; Saffron (chicken gravy); Sage; Spear-
                     mint; Sunflower seeds (fry with bacon and
                     onion for pork chops, pork roast, etc.).

Italian Cuisine: Basil; Black and White Pepper; Capsicum;
(Spaghetti,   Garlic; Kelp; Oregano; Paprika; Saffron (noo-
macaroni,   dles); Sesame seeds (noodles); Turmeric.
pasta, pizza)

Jams, Jellies, Marmalades:	Crab Apple (alone or with pears, plums); Cardamom; Cinnamon; Mace; Peppermint, Spearmint.
Japanese Cuisine:	Burdock root (tempura; sautéed vegetables); Kelp; Onion; Watercress (with water chestnuts and ginger).
Juice: (Fruit)	Allspice; Dandelion leaves and flowers (citrus); Coriander and Lemon Balm (use in orange and grapefruit juice, and lemonade); Peppermint; Spearmint (prune); Slippery Elm (citrus).
Juice: (Vegetable)	Borage; Burdock leaves; Dandelion leaves and flowers; Chives; Capsicum; Kelp; Parsley; Thyme; Slippery Elm (especially good in green drinks).
Mayonnaise:	Chives; Garlic; Saffron; Turmeric; White Pepper.
Meat: (Beef)	Allspice (sweet-sour meat dishes); Angelica (sweetmeats); Basil; Bay; Black Pepper; Capsicum (chili, etc.); Caraway; Celery seed; Chives; Cumin; Coriander (Sage substitute); Garlic; Horseradish (liver, heart, tongue); Kelp; Lovage (stew); Marjoram (stew); Mustard (helps digest beef); Onion; Oregano (meatballs); Paprika; Parsley; Pickling Spice (sauerbraten); Saffron (stew); Savory (barbecue); Sesame seeds; Slippery Elm (keeps fatty meat from becoming rancid); Dandelion root (stew); Tarragon; Thyme (meatloaf).
Meat: (Fish)	Basil; Bay; Black and White Pepper (light fish); Capsicum; Celery seed; Chives; Fennel; Horseradish (seafood relish); Kelp; Lemon Balm (broiled fish); Onion; Paprika; Parsley; Peppermint (trout) Slippery Elm (as a bread-

ing for fried fish); Spearmint (salmon, trout, shrimp, clams, oysters); Tarragon (ingredient in tartar sauce) .

Meat:
(Lamb, mutton)

Allspice; Bay; Black Pepper; Capsicum; Celery seed; Crab Apple (especially mutton); *Dong guei (Tang kuei)*; Garlic; Ginger; Horseradish (Exodus 12:1–8, considered to be one of the five bitter herbs the Lord had the Children of Israel eat at their Passover lamb dinner); Kelp; Lovage (stew); Marjoram (stew); Onion; Slippery Elm (keeps mutton from turning rancid); Thyme; Paprika; Parsley; Peppermint (used fresh with mutton in Ethiopia); Saffron (stew); Savory (barbecue); Sesame seed; Tarragon.

Meat:
(Pork)

Bay; Black Pepper; Capsicum; Caraway; Cloves; Coriander (hot dogs); Crab Apple (use with any fat meat); Garlic; Ginger; Dandelion (bacon); Horseradish (smoked ham); Kelp; Mustard; Onion; Parsley; Pickling Spice (pig's feet, liverwurst); Sesame seed; Slippery Elm (keeps fatty substances, such as pork lard from becoming rancid; also as breading for pork chops); Sunflower seeds (fry with bacon); Tarragon.

Meat:
(Poultry)

Basil; Bay; Black Pepper; Capsicum; Coriander (Sage substitute); Crab Apple (grouse, goose, duck, or any oily bird); Garlic; Ginger; Kelp; Onion; Parsley; Saffron; Sage; Savory (barbecue); Sesame; Slippery Elm (as a breading for fried chicken); Tarragon; Thyme.

Meat:
(Venison,
wild game)

Allspice; Bay; Black Pepper; Capsicum; Cloves; Crab Apple; Celery seed; Cumin (roasted peacock); *Dong guei (Tang kuei)* (game hen); Garlic; Ginger; Coriander; (Sage substitute).

Mexican Cuisine: (Tacos, tamales, enchiladas, etc.)	Capsicum; Chili powder; Coriander; Cumin; Garlic; Kelp; Onion; Oregano; Paprika.
Mushrooms:	Marjoram; Oregano; Sage; Thyme.
Potatoes: (Baked, boiled, fried, mashed, salad)	Basil; White Pepper; Capsicum; Caraway; Celery seed; Chives; Dandelion; Dill; Garlic; Horseradish; Kelp; Onion; Paprika; Parsley; Peppermint; Rosemary; Saffron; Sesame seed; Spearmint; Sunflower; Thyme; Turmeric; Watercress.
Sweet Potatoes: (Yams)	Allspice; Cardamom; Cinnamon; Cloves; Mace; Nutmeg; Pumpkin Pie Spice.
Rice Dishes: (see also Chinese and Far East cuisines)	Basil; Borage; Black and White Pepper; Cumin; Caraway; Curry powder; Chives; Garlic; Kelp; Onion; Parsley; Saffron; Savory; Sesame seed; Turmeric; Watercress.
Salad: (Fresh tossed)	Basil; White Pepper; Borage (first immerse fresh leaves in wine; then strain and shred); Capsicum; Celery seed; Coriander; Dandelion; Dill; Fennel; Garlic; Kelp; Lemon Balm Leaves; Lovage; Marjoram; Mustard (fresh); Onion; Parsley; Peppermint (fresh); Rosemary; Saffron; Sage; Savory; Sesame seed; Spearmint (fresh in potato or tossed salads); Tarragon (fresh); Turmeric; Watercress.
Salad: (Dressings)	Capsicum; Coriander; Kelp; Onion; Paprika; Saffron; Tarragon (French-dressing); Turmeric; Watercress; White Pepper.
Sauces:	Allspice; Basil; Bay; Black and White Pepper (white sauces); Capsicum; Celery seed; Fennel; Garlic; Kelp; Marjoram; Mustard; Nutmeg (cream sauce); Onion; Paprika; Parsley; Peppermint; Rosemary; Slippery Elm (fish sauce); Tarragon; Thyme.

Soups: (Chowders)	Bay; Capsicum; Chives; Dill; Garlic; Celery Seed; Kelp; Lemon Balm; Marjoram; Onion; Paprika; Parsley; Peppermint; Sage; Sesame; Slippery Elm; Tarragon; White Pepper.
Soups: (General)	Allspice; Basil; Bay; Black and White Pepper (cream soups); Borage (vegetable soup, add Anise or Caraway); Burdock root; Capsicum; Chives; Cloves; Coriander (cream and pea soups); Dandelion; Dill; Fennel; Garlic; Ginger; Kelp; Lovage; Oregano; Nutmeg; Onion; Parsley; Peppermint (pea soup); Rosemary; Sesame seed (thick soups); Tarragon; Slippery Elm (broths); Spearmint (pea-bean purees); Watercress.
Stuffing: (Lamb, pork, poultry, wild game)	Bay; Black Pepper; Capsicum; Crab Apple; Chives; Borage; Dandelion; Garlic; Ginger; Kelp; Oregano; Onion; Parsley; Rosemary; Sage; Savory; Spearmint; Thyme.
Vegetables: (Pickled)	Bay; Basil; Celery seed; Coriander; Dandelion; Dill; Fennel; Garlic; Kelp; Lovage; Onion; Pickling Spice; Rosemary; Tarragon; Turmeric.
Vegetables: (Red)	Allspice; Anise; Basil (tomatoes); Capsicum; Caraway; Cumin; Fennel; Ginger; Horseradish; Kelp; Oregano; Paprika; Parsley; Sage (stewed tomatoes); Savory (beets, tomatoes); Sesame seed; Tarragon (tomatoes, beets); Thyme (beets, tomatoes).
Vegetables: (Yellow and orange)	Allspice; Anise; Basil; Cardamom; Cinnamon; Cloves; Fennel; Ginger; Mace; Nutmeg; Peppermint (carrots); Sage (carrots); Savory; Sesame seed; Sunflower seeds (yellow, crookneck and other squash); Thyme (carrots); Turmeric (yellow vegetables that are not sweet).

Vegetables: Dill; Fennel (parsnips); Horseradish (turnips);
(White)   Lovage; Paprika; Rosemary (eggplant); Sage
                 (eggplant); Tarragon (cauliflower); White
                 Pepper.

PART TWO

Alcoholic Beverages: Beer and Wine

Beer is known to have some antiseptic value. The ancients made frequent use of it in their medicines. The noted Harvard pathologist, Dr. Guido Majno, made these observations about the therapeutic benefits of beer:

"The Sumerians were great beer lovers: they brewed at least 19 brands—there is a whole book on the subject. . . . As the antiseptic properties of wine depend on components other than alcohol, it is possible that beer contains such antibacterial substances. . . . Juniper (*Burashu*) later became the most used ingredient of Akkadian pharmacy. . . . The diseased part was first washed with beer and hot water. A Sumerian could scarcely have chosen a better wound-wash."

Wine has great antiseptic value. It was used in ancient times, especially by the Romans, for treating infectious diseases, even acute ones like gangrene. But its wonderful medicinal properties are principally due to the spices employed in the delicate art of wine-making. Dr. Majno discussed the historical aspects of wine:

"The jump from spices to wounds to wine is not as long as it may seem. For wounds and wines, to begin, have the same problem: bacterial infection. And both can be cured by aromatic substances. The main infectious disease of wine is vinegar. So, while the people of antiquity were trying to prevent their wounds from developing what they called 'corruption,' they were also spending enormous amounts of energy in trying to keep their wine from turning into vinegar. The villains, whether staphylococci or aetobacteria, were always microorganisms, and they had to be killed with antiseptics. Consciously or not, our ancestors did make the connection between the two problems, for they discovered that many of the substances that kept wounds clean also kept wine from becoming vinegar, especially the aromata (spices)."

Some of the spices used by the ancients in their wine-making, besides the veteran preservative, Myrrh gum, were Cardamom, Cinnamon, Marjoram, Peppermint, Thyme, Spearmint and Wormwood (Wormwood, by the way, is the word—and the substance—that gave vermouth).

The ancient use of spices in wines greatly influenced the development of modern medicine as Dr. Majno points out:

"Ultimately, man's consuming interest in wine paid off. Much wine had to flow—and much vinegar—until the catharsis came in the 19th century. One great day Napoleon III, heeding the call of distressed French wine makers, looked around for a scientist who could solve their problems, and chose Louis Pasteur. That was July, 1863. Within three years, Pasteur had earned a gold medal for proposing a cheap remedy that was later called pasteurization. Thus, pasteurization was born in wine, not milk." Pasteur's classical book on the *Maladies du Vin*, published in 1866, contains many lovely drawings of bacteria in "diseased wines" (Pasteur discovered that the good yeasts and the vinegar-making bacteria swam side-by-side in wine). The work on human infections that eventually made Pasteur one of the saviors of mankind, the work that inspired Lister's antisepsis, grew from Pasteur's earlier studies on what makes sugar turn to alcohol, and alcohol to vinegar.

It should also be pointed out that Louis Pasteur, as early as 1860, felt that eventually his studies with beer, wine, vinegar and the spices used to make these two alcoholic beverages, would some day lead to more serious research on the origin of infectious diseases in man. Through this brief bit of history we are able to see just how dramatically certain food spices used in the art of beer and wine making greatly influenced and changed the future of modern medicine.

Even more controversial are recent medical and scientific findings that beer and wine can lower serum cholesterol levels in the blood, thereby preventing atherosclerosis and coronary heart disease. One such study was recently published in the *Journal of the American Medical Association (J.A.M.A.)*. The team of Boston doctors doing this research noticed that invariably men who drank small amounts of beer, wine, and liquor each day experienced little or virtually no coronary heart disease;

whereas those who did not drink manifested all kinds of symptoms of heart disease.

In the same issue, a spokesman from the National Heart Institute recommended moderate intake of some alcohol each day for stronger hearts (i.e., two beers; two glasses of wine; two glasses of spirits or two highballs); but cautioned against the dangers of overindulgence. This study is underscored by the importance of several others done with various groups of people throughout the world.

A group of doctors and nutritionists recently studied the health of the Tarahumara Indians of Northern Mexico, who have the distinction of being the fastest runners on earth. Scientists discovered that these modern-day Spartans had lower levels of cholesterol, body fat and saturated fat than did average Americans living in Iowa. Noticeably absent from among the Tarahumaras was any incidence of high blood pressure, obesity, atherosclerosis and coronary heart disease.

Anthropologists and sociologists who have studied these people thoroughly, point out that a fermented corn beer called *tesguino* has a primary functional importance in the social organization and culture, and has a profound influence upon the history of the Tarahumara.

The Indians claim the method and ingredients for brewing this alcoholic beverage was revealed to them by supernatural beings who told them it would keep their people in good health if they frequently consumed it. Whether or not this was providential remains to be seen; yet the medical facts cannot be ignored—the Tarahumaras do not have any clinical signs of coronary heart disease whatsoever!

Add to this the fact that Soviet centenarians (110 and 120 is a common age for many of them) consume moderate to large amounts of beer, wine and vodka daily, and register no heart problems to speak of. We are led to admit that alcoholic beverages do have some therapeutic health value if used in moderation.

Most commercial beers and wines made today contain a host of questionable chemicals that could pose serious health threats to those who imbibe them. When you consider that beer usually contains methanol (a definite poison) and lead (a health hazard) and various nitrites suspected of being carcinogenic, then one begins to appreciate the value of making home-brew instead.

Or how about the traces of arsenic legally allowed in most commercial wines for clarity? More disturbing, though, is the 3 percent solution of hydrogen peroxide used by many manufacturers and distillers to age wine and liquors artificially. An incredibly stronger 90 percent solution is used as one of the principal ingredients in rocket propulsion, while a more modest 30 percent solution is used by heavy industry. Thus, the dinner wine sipped in a quiet French restaurant and the blast-off power beneath our huge Saturn rockets both have something very much in common—hydrogen peroxide!

Herbs which are used to flavor commercial wines include: Angelica, Basil, Cardamom seeds, Cinnamon, Cloves, Curry powder, Ginger, Juniper berries, Lemon Balm, Mace, Marjoram, Oregano, Peppermint, Rosemary, Sage, Summer Savory, Spearmint and Thyme.

Sherry wine requires the sweeter herbs and mild spices. Claret and burgundy require the stronger herbs and medium spices. Sauterne and sweet wines require the pungent spices.

Other herbs used in the making of alcoholic beverages are: Allspice (wine, cordials); Angelica (gin); Anise (in certain liqueurs like anisette and absinthe); Caraway; Juniper (gin); Dandelion (beer, wine); Cumin (German wine); Nutmeg (wine); Spearmint (mint julep with bourbon); and Tarragon (liqueur).

A simple way to prepare herbal commercial wines is to steep the aromatic herb (herbs) in a white wine (better if you make your own) for three to four days. Cover and allow the mixture to remain in a warm place, as in the preparation of a herb vinegar. Stir daily. Strain through absorbent cotton or filter paper and bottle. Label the ingredients.

PART THREE

A Survey of Plant Oils

A recent survey of plant oils revealed that experiments with laboratory animals and humans indicate that plant sterols may decrease the absorption of dietary and endogenous cholesterol. High phytosterol intake has also been associated with lowering of blood cholesterol in man.

This same report showed that Sesame seed oil was one of the highest in total plant sterols. For 100 grams of the oil, there is a total of 2,950 total plant sterols, (more than Sunflower, Safflower, olive and wheat germ oils).

Of the spices mentioned in this book having phytosterols, those with the highest amounts are: Anise, Basil, Clove, Dill, Fenugreek, White Mustard, Oregano, Paprika, Sage (Coriander, a Sage-substitute, surprisingly is very low), and Thyme.

While Garlic itself is rather low in phytosterols, there are other factors in Garlic oil that makes it ideal for lowering serum cholesterol and preventing atherosclerosis. Rabbits fed high-cholesterol diets and then administered daily doses of Garlic showed remarkably low cholesterol content in their heart aortas and livers.

Sesame seed oil is also great for staph infection, as a leading pathologist noted: oil was a common dressing in ancient times; presumably with Sesame oil in Mesopotamia, Olive oil in Palestine. Oil and grease cannot do much harm on raw flesh, and they also serve the useful purpose of preventing the bandage from sticking to the wound, like today's first-aid creams. Bacteria do not grow in oil. In fact, we tested the survival of staphylococci in Sesame oil and found that they were rapidly killed.

Besides Sesame, Sunflower, Bay, and Garlic oils, White Pepper, Chives, and Onion may be added to plant oils for flavor. Annatto can be added for coloring. On the other hand, Ginger, Turmeric, and especially Slippery Elm bark may be added to plant and animal oils to increase their shelf life and keep them from going rancid.

Food scientists at Rutgers University in New Jersey, headed by Dr. Stephen Chang, have made the discovery that distilled extracts of Rosemary and Sage can act as antioxidants in helping to preserve the cooking integrity of shortening and salad oils. They feel that these two herbs will one day replace the artificial preservatives now used—BHT and BHA.

The nordihydroguaiaretic acid or NDGA in Chaparral has also been used extensively throughout the food industry as a preservative for a number of items, from meat to cooking oils.

The Swift Meat Company has tested a number of herbs within recent years, both culinary as well as medicinal, for their antibiotic effects in preserving certain processed foods. Among the herbs successfully tested and used for this purpose have been Iris bulbs, dry Sage, Canadian Thistle (pickling solutions), Avocado tree and root (luncheon meats and cured meats and hams), common Agrimony, purple Prairie Clover, St. Johnswort and Iceland moss.

PART FOUR

Reducing Salt (Sodium) Intake with Herbs and Spices

Millions of Americans today are on salt-free, sodium-restricted diets. They must often contend with bland and nearly tasteless foods in order to obtain the proper nutrition which their bodies require. But some helpful advice to eliminate such problems comes from Dr. Judith Wylie-Rosett, director of the nutrition division at the Department of Community Health of the Albert Einstein College of Medicine in New York City. She suggests using generous amounts of various culinary spices in order to give foods flavorful zest. Among her recommendations are the following:

(1) Use Onion and Garlic powder in place of bouillon cubes or instant packaged soups. Make homemade broths using dehydrated mixed vegetable flakes.

(2) When making sandwiches use lettuce, cucumber and tomato for moisture rather than prepared mayonnaise. Sprinkle the vegetables with herbs to replace the missing flavor from the dressing.

(3) Before roasting or broiling chicken, rub with lemon juice and herbs, or poultry seasoning. The same with fish.

(4) Bottled salad dressings are high in sodium. Instead, combine lemon juice or vinegar, herbs, and a bit of oil. Shake well in a covered jar.

(5) For lovers of Southern cooking, cook greens with a beef bone instead of a ham bone. Season with plenty of Black Pepper (note: I suggest Capsicum instead).

(6) When entertaining, dips can be made from yogurt flavored with Dill weed, Garlic and Onion powders. Fresh vegetables are good dippers. Puffed wheat or rice, seasoned with unsalted Chili powder or Garlic and Onion powders, may be toasted in the oven or heated in a non-stick pan. Popcorn is

another good food for entertaining. Don't add salt—use Garlic or Onion powder instead.

(7) For a sausage flavor in spaghetti sauce, combine fresh tomato sauce (or use canned, unsalted tomatoes) with such typical sausage herbs as Fennel, Basil, Pepper, and Onion and Garlic powders.

(8) Brown rice, bulghur (cracked wheat) and kasha (buckwheat) are recommended. They have more taste—and nutritive value—than the refined wheat products, and they accept seasoning for variety very well. Try Curry powder, Italian seasoning (blend), poultry seasoning and, for a surprise, a touch of Cinnamon.

(9) When dining in a restaurant: Order, if possible, individually-broiled items such as chicken, chops or fish and tell the waiter that they should not be salted. Make up little cards which can be given directly to the chef: "Sprinkle with Oregano and lemon juice. Please do not salt."

(10) Make herbal packets to take along when dining out.

An added word of caution: Kelp should *not* be used by those on sodium-restricted diets, since the herb is incredibly high in this mineral.

PART FIVE

Successful Sprouting

With the current popularity being enjoyed by sprouts in the health food movement, some food technologists with certain universities have decided to investigate the chemical composition and nutritive food value of various kinds of sprouts. A summary of their findings was written up in a leading journal of food science:

"Sprouting of grains caused increased enzyme activity, a loss of total dry matter, an increase in total protein, a change in amino acid composition, a decrease in starch, increases in sugars, a slight increase in crude fat and crude fiber, and slightly higher amounts of certain vitamins and minerals." The report gave some interesting information in detail. For example, certain amino acids experienced an increase in sprouts as the following table indicates.

	barley		oats		rye		wheat		triticale	
Amino acid	grain	sprouts	grain	sprouts	grain	sprouts	grain	sprouts	grain	sprouts
lysine	2.9	5.5	3.6	6.4	3.1	4.8	2.4	5.7	2.6	4.8
histidine	1.8	2.2	2.1	2.5	2.0	1.8	2.2	2.1	2.0	11.8
ammonia	3.3	4.3	3.2	3.6	3.5	4.2	3.9	4.2	3.4	4.7
arginine	4.9	5.2	6.9	5.3	4.9	4.7	4.1	5.2	5.0	5.1
aspartic acid	6.3	23.1	9.8	18.3	7.5	21.5	5.0	24.1	6.5	26.2
threonine	3.3	3.9	3.5	4.2	3.1	3.3	2.6	3.6	2.9	3.6
serine	4.1	4.0	4.9	4.2	4.2	3.5	4.2	3.7	4.2	3.8

(grams per 100 grams amino acid recovered)

Table 1. Amino acid levels of grains compared with sprouts.

Changes in mineral elements during the sprouting of wheat was also rather interesting. While a few dropped slightly, others increased a bit.

Days of sprouting	calcium	iron	zinc	magnesium
0	34.9	4.12	2.79	169.4
3	35.7	3.50	2.90	160.3
4	36.0	3.54	2.99	164.7
5	39.6	4.02	3.36	166.6

Table 2. Changes in mineral content of wheat during first five days. Changes in mineral content of barley and barley sprouts were even more dramatic. The barley was steeped to 45 percent water at 16° C and malted at 16° Centigrade for 7 days to get the sprouts obtained.

Mineral	Barley	Barley sprouts
phosphorus	3,160	5,960
potassium	4,570	22,080
magnesium	1,360	1,500
calcium	259	692
iron	26.1	55.9
zinc	20.1	84.9
manganese	14.9	45.1
copper	4.2	15.5

Table 3. Comparison of mineral content of barley grain and sprouts. SOURCE: Klaus Lorenz, "Cereal Sprouts: Composition, Nutritive Value, Food Applications," *Critical Reviews in Food Science and Nutrition*, 13:353–385, December 1980.

Food technologists elsewhere in the country have noticed vitamin increases in various kinds of germinated wheat. Below we can see the effects which sprouting has on the carotene (pro-vitamin A) content of five classes of wheat. Vitamin A equivalents are given per pound of wheat used.

	Days of sprouting		
Class of wheat	0	3	7
hard red spring	300	300	400
soft white	300	500	500
soft red winter	400	400	400
durum	300	400	400
hard red winter	100	400	600

Table 4. Carotene content in wheat sprouts
SOURCE: B.F. Miller, *Proceedings of the 10th National Conference on Wheat Utilization Research*; Tucson, November 1977; p. 144.

Ann Wigmore, founder of the Hippocrates Health Institute in Boston, Massachusetts, has made something of an art and science out of sprouting. She uses powdered herbs in equal parts, for example, as the ingredients for an activator used in composting. This compost, in turn, is used to grow Wheatgrass, Sunflower greens, and Buckwheat lettuce for sprouting purposes. The powdered herbs, used in equal parts, are: wild Chamomile; Dandelion; Valerian; Yarrow; Stinging Nettle; and Oak bark. Pure honey is added.

Ordinarily we may just think of Wheatgrass or mung bean and Alfalfa sprouts. However, this lady in Boston has added a few spice herbs to the sprouting list. They are: Dill; Fenugreek; Mustard; Sesame seed; Sunflower and Watercress.

Brief instructions for the preparation of each:

Dill: eight hours (soaking time); three times/day fill with water, rinse, drain; three to five days (average harvest time); great with salads, sandwiches, juices.

Fenugreek: Same as for Dill but special handling is required; mist gently with water. Good with salads, snacks.

Mustard: No special soaking time required; three times/day fill with water, rinse, drain; three to five days (average harvest time); special handling (mist or finely spray with water three times per day or mix with other seeds); good with salads and juices.

Sesame: Eight hours (soaking time); three times/day fill with water, rinse, drain; two to three days (average harvest time); good in breads, granola, and snacks.

Sunflower: Same as above, except that average harvest time is one to two days; and that the hulls need to be removed before sprouting commences. Use in salads, snacks.

Watercress: No soaking time and fill/rinse/drain water procedures needed. Average harvest time is three to five days. Does require special handling (spray with gentle water mist three times per day or mix with other seeds). Ideal in salads, sandwiches, breads, soups.

General Directions for Sprouting

From Ann Wigmore's Institute comes the following method of sprouting:

Time and temperature determine when a seed reaches maturity. In warm weather soak seeds less, and rinse more frequently to keep them cool. Your sprouts will mature more quickly in warm weather. In colder weather, soak seeds longer, rinse less frequently; they will take longer to mature. 70° F. is the right temperature for most seeds.

Basically, care of sprouts means keeping them moist, and providing adequate drainage. Another tip: wash seeds thoroughly before soaking. Do this by rinsing the seeds a few times, and swishing them around gently in the bottle. If at all feasible, soak your seeds in spring or purified water. "Sprouts respond to your energy. Give them love and they will love your body," claims Ann Wigmore.

Instructions for rinsing:
Spread the rinsing time out as evenly as possible. If done twice a day, rinse early in the morning and late in the afternoon. For three times a day, rinse first thing in the morning, again at 2:00 p.m. or so, and last thing before retiring at night.

To rinse, stand the jar upright. Let the water fill the jar. As it does you will see a ring of foam rise to the top. Let the water overflow and carry the foam away. The foam contains the waste products of the sprouts.

Turn the jar upside down; keep it tilted at an angle so that the air can pass in and out of the opening. Try to make sure the sprouts do not cover the opening completely.

Seeds do not need to be de-hulled during the sprouting process. If you want to, however, simply skim the loose and broken hulls off the surface of the water as you rinse the sprouts. They are lighter in weight than the main body of sprouts, and will rise to the top of the jar as a part of the ring of foam. Scoop them out of the jar with your hand.

An alternative method: Gently turn the sprouts into a basin filled with water. Swish the body of sprouts around so that the loose hulls float off. Push the main body of sprouts under the water with your hand or a screen; skim the hulls off the surface of the water.

Alfalfa, Radish, Red Clover and mung respond well to de-hulling. Fenugreek and lentils don't need it.

Allow your sprouts to rest and grow in a quiet, peaceful corner, with little or no sunlight. Place Alfalfa in the sun after five or six days.

SECTION THREE

Nutritional and Botanical Information

This section contains the following information about the herbs and spices used in this book: protein, fat, crude fiber, vitamin and mineral content; and chemical constituents (oils, acids, alkaloids, etc.).

For ease of reference, this information has been arranged into appropriate tables and charts, each of which explains the data presented, and how to read and interpret it.

PART ONE

Protein, Fat and Crude Fiber Content of Herbs and Spices

Protein
The protein content of the spice herbs listed ranged from 4 to 26 percent. Especially at the middle and high ends of the range, the amounts were comparable to those found in grains, such as oats (14.2 percent protein) and wheat (9–14 percent protein) and in mature dry beans (2–23 percent protein), but were less than the 34 percent protein of soybeans.

Spices from seeds were higher in protein than those from other parts of the plant. The low value in the range for protein from seeds was for Nutmeg (6 percent). The protein of the other three seed-origin spices ranged from Poppy seeds (18 percent) to Sesame seeds (26 percent). Several leaves were among the spices highest in protein, with 20 percent or more protein. These included Coriander leaves, Dill weed, Parsley and Tarragon. Spices from bark were the lowest in protein.

Fat:
Spices from seeds (i.e. Nutmeg, Mustard, Poppy, Sesame) were much higher in fat than those from other groups. In fact, the Mustard seed, having the lowest average fat content (29 percent) was higher than any of the spices from other groups except Mace (32 percent fat). Celery seed and Cumin of fruit origin were also near to Mace (25 and 22 percent fat, respectively).

Fiber:
Spices generally were very high in fiber (2–29 percent). In comparison, mature dry beans contain about 4 percent fiber and wheat grain, 2 percent. Spices from seeds and from bulbs or roots had lower fiber contents than the other groups. Spices from bark were high in fiber. Kelp is especially high in fiber

content. *For those concerned about fiber in their diets, spices are definitely worth investigating.*

Contents for protein, fat, crude fiber and minerals is given in two sets of percentage figures—an average number and the low-and-high range for each spice.

Leaves
Basil, Bay leaf, Coriander leaf, Dill weed, Marjoram, Oregano, Rosemary, Sage, Savory, Tarragon, Thyme.

Protein		*Fat*		*crude Fiber*	
average (%)	range	average (%)	range	average (%)	range
14	5–23	7	4–15	15	7–26

Fruits
Allspice, Anise, Caraway, Cardamom, Celery seed, Coriander seed, Cumin, Dill seed, Fennel seed, Mace, Paprika, Pepper (Black, White, Red, Capsicum).

14	6–20	15	2–32	15	4–29

Seeds
Mustard, Nutmeg, Poppy, Sesame.

19	6–26	41	20–55	5	3–7

Bulbs & Roots
Garlic, Ginger, Onion, Turmeric.

11	8–17	4	1–10	5	2–7

Bark
Cinnamon

4	—	3	—	24	—

	Calcium		Magnesium		Phosphorus		Iron		Sodium		Potassium	
	average	range	average	range	average	range	average	range	average	range	average	range
					milligrams/100 grams							
Leaves: Basil, Bay leaf, Coriander leaf, Dill weed, Marjoram, Oregano, Rosemary, Sage, Savory, Tarragon, Thyme.												
	1,575	835–2,130	330	120–695	290	70–545	53	28–124	100	10–450	2,335	530–4,740
Fruits: Allspice, Anise, Caraway, Cardamom, Celery seed, Coriander seed, Cumin, Dill seed, Fennel, Mace, Paprika, Pepper (3).												
	700	150–1,770	240	90–440	330	110–570	23	7–66	55	5–170	1,320	75–2,345
Seeds: Mustard, Nutmeg, Poppy, Sesame.												
	570	130–1,450	290	185–345	670	215–850	8	3–10	20	5–40	535	350–700
Bulbs and Roots: Garlic, Ginger, Onion, Turmeric.												
	185	80–365	140	60–195	295	150–415	15	3–41	40	25–55	1,480	945–2,525
Bark: Cinnamon.												
	1,230	—	55	—	60	—	38	—	25	—	500	—

Table 6. Mineral Content of Herbs

SOURCES: Elizabeth W. Murphy et al, "Nutrient Content of Spices and Herbs"; *Journ. of the American Dietetic Assoc.* 72:174–176, Feb. 1978. Consumer & Food Economics Institute, *Seasoning With Spices and Herbs*; USDA CA 62–24 Agriculture Research Service, Sept. 1972. A.C. Marsh et al, *Composition of Foods: Spices and Herbs—Raw, Processed, Prepared*; USDA Agricultural Handbook No. 8–2, 1977.

PART TWO

A Summary of
Mineral Content of Herbs and Spices

The survey of the mineral content of herbs and spices showed that leaves were high in both calcium and magnesium compared with other groups of herbs and spices. Fruits and seeds were also high. Spices from bulbs and roots were rather low in both minerals, while those from bark were high in calcium, but lowest in magnesium. Within the groups, a wide range of values was found for these two minerals.

For example, the calcium content of leaves ranged from 835 mg per 100 gms for Bay leaf, to more than 2,100 mg per 100 gm for Basil and Savory. For spices of fruit origin, magnesium values ranged from 90 to 440 mg per 100 gm of White Pepper and Celery seed, respectively. Most of the leaf, fruit and seed spices contained 200 mg per 100 gm.

The average phosphorus content of the seed group was at least twice of any other group. Within this group, however, Nutmeg was by far the lowest, containing an average of 215 mg phosphorus per 100 mg. In comparison, the other seeds— Mustard, Poppy and Sesame—which were high in phosphorus, with 400 mg or more per 100 gm. These spices, although called seeds, were actually the fruits of the plant. Spices from bark were very much lower in phosphorus than those of the other groups.

Average iron content was from two to six times higher in leaves than in other groups. Although a range of 28 mg in Sage to 124 mg in Thyme was found, most values for iron in leaves tended to cluster in the range between 30 and 50 mg per 100 gm. Other spices ranged from a low of about 3 mg iron in Garlic and Onion and Nutmeg, to a high of 66 mg in Cumin.

Leaves were highest of all groups in sodium and potassium. Spices from seeds were low in both sodium and potassium, in comparison with other groups, while those of bulb or root origin were relatively low in sodium and high in potassium. Considerable variability within a group was found for both minerals, especially for potassium. For instance, potassium in spices of fruit origin ranged from 75 mg for White Pepper to 2,345 mg per 100 gm of Paprika.

The highest average value for sodium in leaves shown on the mineral table on the preceding page is largely due to the values of Coriander leaves and Dill weed at 210 mg per 100 gm. In contrast, Bay leaf, Oregano, Sage, and Savory all contained less than 25 mg sodium per 100 gm.

Among spices from fruiting parts, White Pepper, Cardamom seed, Anise and Caraway were low in sodium, with less than 20 mg, while Celery seed and Cumin were much higher, containing 160 and 170 mg sodium per 100 gm, respectively. Another spice relatively high in sodium was Cloves, with approximately 245 mg per 100 gm. The sodium content of most spices ranged between 5 and 90 mg per gm.

Spices are usually used in small amounts in foods. For instance, the U.S. measure of 1 teaspoon weighs about two grams for many spices. Thus, the contribution to the daily requirement of nutrients would be small for most spices. However, a few spices were relatively high in sodium, even in 2-gram amounts. These include Celery seed, Cumin, Coriander leaf, Dill weed, and Cloves, which ranged from 3 to 5 mg sodium in 2 gm of spice. (Note: Although not listed on the mineral table with the rest of the spices, but placed separately with several others on the following pages, Parsley flakes are very high in sodium—9 mg per 2 gm.) For diets in which sodium is restricted, such as the 250 mg and 500 mg sodium diets described by the American Heart Association, spices with lower sodium contents might be preferred as seasonings.

In today's society most of us have come to rely upon mineral and vitamin supplements to provide us with the important nutrients which our daily food doesn't seem capable of supplying.

The use of spices can support the work of supplements; spices are aromatic and flavorsome herbs designed to improve both the taste and nutritional qualities of the foods with which they are used. By utilizing them more often we will be cooperating with Nature in getting our nutrients from the food we eat and not only from capsule/tablet sources.

PART THREE

Vitamin and Mineral Content of Herbs and Spices

Column A lists the individual herb/spice, followed by the heading for the minerals, vitamins and, in some cases, the amino acids they contain. Columns B and C are the values of mineral and vitamin content, expressed in milligrams, for one teaspoon and one tablespoon of the spice. Those vitamins measured in micrograms are so noted with the abbreviation mcg.

SPICES Minerals (mg) Vitamins (mg) A	Amount in edible portion of common measures of food (mg) Approx. measure & weight 1 tsp = 1.9 g B	1 tbsp = 6.0 g C
ALLSPICE		
calcium	13	40
iron	.13	.42
magnesium	3	8
phosphorus	2	7
potassium	20	63
sodium	1	5
zinc	.02	.06
ascorbic acid	.75	2.35
thiamine	.002	.006
riboflavin	.001	.004
niacin	.054	.172
pantothenic acid	———	———
vitamin B6	———	———
folacin (mcg)	———	———
vitamin B12 (mcg)	0	0
vitamin A (IU)	10	32

	1 tsp = 1.9 g	1 tbsp = 6.0 g
ANISE SEED		
calcium	14	43
iron	.78	2.48
magnesium	4	11
phosphorus	9	29
potassium	30	97
sodium	Trace	1
zinc	.11	.36

Vitamin contents unknown
CHINESE ANGELICA (DONG GUEI, TANG KUEI)
Vitamin A retinoids; B-12; considerable E; and minimal amounts of cobalt.

BASIL		
calcium	30	95
iron	.59	1.89
magnesium	6	19
phosphorus	7	22
potassium	48	154
sodium	Trace	2
zinc	.98	.26
ascorbic acid	.86	2.76
thiamine	.002	.007
riboflavin	.004	.014
niacin	.097	.313
pantothenic acid	———	———
vitamin B6	———	———
folacin (mcg)	———	———
vitamin B12 (mcg)	0	0
vitamin A (IU)	131	422

Amino Acid (grams)		
tryptophan	.003	.010
threonine	.008	.026
isoleucine	.008	.026
leucine	.015	.049
lysine	.009	.028
methionine	.003	.009
cystine	.002	.007
phenylalanine	.010	.033

	1 tsp = 1.9 g	1 tbsp = 6.0 g
tryosine	.006	.019
valine	.010	.032
arginine	.009	.030
histidine	.004	.013
alanine	.010	.034
aspartic acid	.024	.076
glutamic acid	.022	.070
glycine	.010	.031
proline	.008	.026
serine	.008	.025

BAY LEAF

calcium	5	15
iron	.26	.77
magnesium	1	2
phosphorus	1	2
potassium	3	10
sodium	Trace	Trace
zinc	.02	.07
ascorbic acid	.28	.84
thiamine	Trace	Trace
riboflavin	.003	.008
niacin	.012	.036
pantothenic acid	——	——
vitamin B6	——	——
folacin	——	——
vitamin B12	0	0

CARAWAY SEED

calcium	14	46
iron	.34	1.09
magnesium	5	17
phosphorus	12	38
potassium	28	91
sodium	Trace	1
zinc	.12	.37
ascorbic acid	——	——
thiamine	.008	.026
riboflavin	.008	.025
niacin	.076	.242
pantothenic acid	——	——

	1 tsp = 1.9 g	1 tbsp = 6.0 g
vitamin B6	——	——
folacin (mcg)	——	——
vitamin B12 (mcg)	0	0
vitamin A (IU)	8	24
CARDAMOM		
calcium	8	22
iron	.28	.81
magnesium	5	13
phosphorus	4	10
potassium	22	65
sodium	Trace	1
zinc	.15	.43
ascorbic acid	——	——
thiamine	.004	.011
riboflavin	.004	.011
niacin	.022	.064
pantothenic acid	——	——
vitamin B6	——	——
folacin (mcg)	——	——
vitamin B12 (mcg)	0	0
vitamin A (IU)		
CELERY SEED		
calcium	35	115
iron	.90	2.92
magnesium	9	29
phosphorus	11	36
potassium	28	91
sodium	3	10
zinc	.14	.45
ascorbic acid	.34	1.11
thiamine	——	——
riboflavin	——	——
niacin	——	——
pantothenic acid	——	——
vitamin B6	——	——
folacin (mcg)	——	——
vitamin B12 (mcg)	0	0
vitamin A (IU)	1	3

	1 tsp = 1.9 g	1 tbsp = 6.0 g
CHILI POWDER		
(cayenne, cumin, oregano, salt, garlic powder)		
calcium	7	21
iron	.37	1.07
magnesium	4	13
phosphorus	8	23
potassium	50	144
sodium	26	76
zinc	.07	.20
ascorbic acid	1.67	4.81
thiamine	.009	.026
riboflavin	.021	.060
niacin	.205	.592
pantothenic acid	——	——
vitamin B6	——	——
folacin (mcg)	——	——
vitamin B12 (mcg)	0	0
vitamin A (IU)	980	2,620
CINNAMON		
calcium	28	84
iron	.88	2.59
magnesium	1	4
phosphorus	1	4
potassium	11	34
sodium	1	2
zinc	.05	.13
ascorbic acid	.65	1.94
thiamine	.002	.005
riboflavin	.003	.010
niacin	.030	.088
pantothenic acid	——	——
vitamin B6	——	——
folacin (mcg)	——	——
vitamin B12 (mcg)	——	——
vitamin A (IU)	6	18
CORIANDER LEAF		
calcium	7	22
iron	.25	.76
magnesium	4	12

	1 tsp = 1.9 g	1 tbsp = 6.0 g
phosphorus	3	9
potassium	27	80
sodium	1	4
zinc	———	———
ascorbic acid	3.40	10.20
thiamine	.008	.023
riboflavin	.009	.027
niacin	.064	.193
pantothenic acid	———	———
vitamin B6	———	———
folacin (mcg)	———	———
vitamin B12 (mcg)	0	0
vitamin A (IU)	———	———

CORIANDER SEED

	1 tsp = 1.9 g	1 tbsp = 6.0 g
calcium	13	35
iron	.29	.82
magnesium	6	17
phosphorus	7	20
potassium	23	63
sodium	1	2
zinc	.08	.24
ascorbic acid	———	———
thiamine	.004	.012
riboflavin	.005	.014
niacin	.038	.106
pantothenic acid	———	———
vitamin B6	———	———
folacin (mcg)	———	———
vitamin B12 (mcg)	0	0
vitamin A (IU)		

CUMIN SEED

	1 tsp = 1.9 g	1 tbsp = 6.0 g
calcium	20	56
iron	1.39	3.98
magnesium	8	22
phosphorus	10	30
potassium	38	107
sodium	4	10
zinc	.10	.29
ascorbic acid	.16	.46

	1 tsp = 1.9 g	1 tbsp = 6.0 g
thiamine	.013	.038
riboflavin	.007	.020
niacin	.096	.275
pantothenic acid	———	———
vitamin B6	———	———
folacin (mcg)	———	———
vitamin B12 (mcg)	0	0
vitamin A (IU)	27	76

CURRY POWDER
(coriander seed, turmeric,
cumin, fenugreek seed,
white pepper, allspice,
yellow mustard, cayenne,
ginger)

calcium	10	30
iron	.59	1.86
magnesium	5	16
phosphorus	7	22
potassium	31	97
sodium	1	3
zinc	.08	.26
ascorbic acid	.23	.72
thiamine	.005	.016
riboflavin	.006	.018
niacin	.069	.218
pantothenic acid	———	———
vitamin B6	———	———
folacin (mcg)	———	———
vitamin B12 (mcg)	0	0
vitamin A (IU)	20	62

DILL SEED

calcium	32	100
iron	.34	1.08
magnesium	5	17
phosphorus	6	18
potassium	25	78
sodium	Trace	1
zinc	.11	.34
ascorbic acid	———	———

	1 tsp = 1.9 g	1 tbsp = 6.0 g
thiamine	.009	.028
riboflavin	.006	.019
niacin	.059	.185
pantothenic acid	——	——
vitamin B6	——	——
folacin (mcg)	——	——
vitamin B12 (mcg)	0	0
vitamin A (IU)	1	3

Amino Acids (grams)

tryptophan	——	——
threonine	.012	.038
isoleucine	.016	.051
leucine	.019	.061
lysine	.022	.068
methionine	.003	.009
cystine	——	——
phenylalanine	.014	.044
tyrosine	——	——
valine	.024	.074
arginine	.027	.083
histidine	.007	.021

DILL WEED

calcium	18	55
iron	.49	1.51
magnesium	5	14
phosphorus	5	17
potassium	33	103
sodium	2	6
zinc	.03	.10
ascorbic acid	——	——
thiamine	.004	.013
riboflavin	.003	.009
niacin	.029	.086
pantothenic acid	——	——
vitamin B6	.015	.045
folacin (mcg)	——	——
vitamin B12 (mcg)	0	0
vitamin A (IU)	——	——

DANDELION
Raw leaves (one pound) 848 mg calcium; 299 mg phospho-
            (454 grams) rus; 14.1 mg iron; 345 mg sodium
                         1,801 mg potassium; 63,500 I.U.
                         (vitamin A); .86 mg thiamine; 1.18
                         mg riboflavin, 159 mg ascorbic acid
                         (vitamin C).

DONG GUEI (TANG KUEI): See CHINESE ANGELICA.

	1 tsp = 1.9 g	1 tbsp = 6.0 g
FENNEL SEED		
calcium	24	69
iron	.37	1.07
magnesium	8	22
phosphorus	10	28
potassium	34	98
sodium	2	5
zinc	.07	.21
ascorbic acid	———	———
thiamine	.008	.024
riboflavin	.007	.020
niacin	.121	.351
pantothenic acid	———	———
vitamin B6	———	———
folacin (mcg)	———	———
vitamin B12 (mcg)	0	0
vitamin A (IU)	3	8
Amino Acids (grams)		
tryptophan	.005	.015
threonine	.012	.035
isoleucine	.014	.040
leucine	.020	.058
lysine	.015	.044
methionine	.006	.017
cystine	.004	.013
phenylalanine	.013	.038
tyrosine	.008	.024
valine	.018	.053
arginine	.014	.039
histidine	.007	.019

	1 tsp = 1.9 g	1 tbsp = 6.0 g
alanine	.016	.046
aspartic acid	.037	.106
glutamic acid	.059	.171
glycine	.022	.064
proline	.018	.052
serine	.018	.052

FENUGREEK SEED

	1 tsp = 1.9 g	1 tbsp = 6.0 g
calcium	6	19
iron	1.24	3.72
magnesium	7	21
phosphorus	11	33
potassium	28	85
sodium	2	7
zinc	.09	.28
ascorbic acid	.11	.33
thiamine	.012	.036
riboflavin	.014	.041
niacin	.061	.182
pantothenic acid	———	———
vitamin B6	———	———
folacin (mcg)	2.109	6.327
vitamin B12 (mcg)	0	0
vitamin A (IU)	———	———

Amino Acids (grams)

	1 tsp = 1.9 g	1 tbsp = 6.0 g
tryptophan	.014	.043
threonine	.033.	.100
isoleucine	.046	.138
leucine	.065	.195
lysine	.062	.187
methionine	.013	.038
cystine	.014	.041
phenylalanine	.040	.121
tyrosine	.028	.085
valine	.041	.122
arginine	.091	.274
histidine	.025	.074
alanine	.038	.113
aspartic acid	.100	.301
glutamic acid	.148	.443

	1 tsp = 1.9 g	1 tbsp = 6.0 g
glycine	.048	.145
proline	.044	.133
serine	.045	.135

GARLIC POWDER

calcium	2	7
iron	.08	.23
magnesium	2	5
phosphorus	12	35
potassium	31	93
sodium	1	2
zinc	.07	.22
ascorbic acid	———	———
thiamine	.013	.039
riboflavin	.004	.013
niacin	.019	.058
pantothenic acid	———	———
vitamin B6	———	———
folacin (mcg)	———	———
vitamin B12 (mcg)	0	0
vitamin A (IU)		

Amino Acids (grams)

tryptophan	.006	.018
threonine	.013	.039
isoleucine	.018	.054
leucine	.029	.086
lysine	.016	.049
methionine	.009	.028
cystine	.005	.014
phenylalanine	.014	.041
tyrosine	.006	.018
valine	.020	.060
arginine	.047	.141
histidine	.009	.026
alanine	.010	.029
aspartic acid	.036	.108
glutamic acid	.060	.179
glycine	.015	.044
proline	.007	.022
serine	.014	.042

	1 tsp = 1.9 g	1 tbsp = 6.0 g
GINGER		
calcium	2	6
iron	.21	.62
magnesium	3	10
phosphorus	3	8
potassium	24	68
sodium	1	2
zinc	.08	.25
ascorbic acid	———	———
thiamine	.001	.002
riboflavin	.003	.010
niacin	.093	.278
pantothenic acid	———	———
vitamin B6	———	———
folacin (mcg)	———	———
vitamin B12 (mcg)	0	0
vitamin A (IU)	3	8
Amino Acids (grams)		
tryptophan	.001	.003
threonine	.003	.010
isoleucine	.005	.014
leucine	.007	.021
lysine	.005	.016
methionine	.001	.004
cystine	.001	.002
phenylalanine	.004	.013
tyrosine	.002	.006
valine	.007	.021
arginine	.004	.012
histidine	.003	.009
alanine	.003	.009
aspartic acid	.020	.059
glutamic acid	.015	.046
glycine	.004	.012
proline	.004	.012
serine	.004	.013

HORSERADISH
1 teaspoon: 3 mg calcium; 2 mg phosphorus; trace of iron;
                5 mg sodium; 15 mg potassium

1 tablespoon: 9 mg calcium; 5 mg phosphorus; .1 mg iron;
                14 mg sodium; 44 mg potassium

KELP (powdered seaweed)
Vitamins: A, B, D and E.
Minerals: Calcium, potassium, and sodium (10 percent
                    of kelp ash), iodine (3 percent).
Trace Elements: Aluminum, iron, magnesium, strontium,
                    copper, tin, lead, vanadium, zinc, barium,
                    chromium, titanium manganese, silver, sili-
                    con (not soluble in sea water yet found in
                    kelp).
Other factors: fructose (a sugar not harmful to diabetics),
                    carbohydrate (starch), fats, protein.

Note: If root vegetables were burned only 1 percent mineral ash
remains; but if kelp is burned, 10–50 percent remains as mineral ash.

	1 tsp = 1.9 g	1 tbsp = 6.0 g
MACE		
calcium	4	13
iron	.24	.74
magnesium	3	9
phosphorus	2	6
potassium	8	25
sodium	1	4
zinc	.04	.12
ascorbic acid	———	———
thiamine	.005	.017
riboflavin	.008	.024
niacin	.023	.072
pantothenic acid	———	———
vitamin B6	———	———
folacin (mcg)	———	———
vitamin B12 (mcg)	0	0
vitamin A (IU)	14	42
MARJORAM		
calcium	12	34
iron	.50	1.41
magnesium	2	6

	1 tsp = 1.9 g	1 tbsp = 6.0 g
phosphorus	2	5
potassium	9	26
sodium	Trace	1
zinc	.02	.06
ascorbic acid	.31	.87
thiamine	.002	.005
riboflavin	.002	.005
niacin	.025	.070
pantothenic acid	————	————
vitamin B6	————	————
folacin (mcg)	————	————
vitamin B12 (mcg)	0	0
vitamin A (IU)	48	137

MUSTARD SEED

calcium	17	58
iron	.33	1.12
magnesium	10	33
phosphorus	28	94
potassium	23	76
sodium	Trace	1
zinc	.19	.64
ascorbic acid	————	————
thiamine	.018	.061
riboflavin	.013	.043
niacin	.260	.884
pantothenic acid	————	————
vitamin B6	————	————
folacin (mcg)	————	————
vitamin B12 (mcg)	0	0
vitamin A (IU)	2	7

Amino Acids (grams)

tryptophan	.017	.059
threonine	.036	.123
isoleucine	.036	.121
leucine	.059	.200
lysine	.050	.170
methionine	.016	.054
cystine	.019	.065
phenylalanine	.035	.119

	1 tsp = 1.9 g	1 tbsp = 6.0 g
tyrosine	.025	.083
valine	.044	.148
arginine	.058	.196
histidine	.025	.085
alanine	.039	.133
aspartic acid	.065	.220
glutamic acid	.164	.558
glycine	.043	.147
proline	.064	.218
serine	.036	.121

NUTMEG

calcium	4	13
iron	.07	.21
magnesium	4	13
phosphorus	5	15
potassium	8	24
sodium	Trace	1
zinc	.05	.15
ascorbic acid	———	———
thiamine	.008	.024
riboflavin	.001	.004
niacin	.029	.091
pantothenic acid	———	———
vitamin B6	———	———
folacin (mcg)	———	———
vitamin B12 (mcg)	0	0
vitamin A (IU)	2	7

ONION POWDER

calcium	8	24
iron	.05	.17
magnesium	3	8
phosphorus	7	22
potassium	20	61
sodium	1	3
zinc	.05	.15
ascorbic acid	.31	.95
thiamine	.009	.027
riboflavin	.001	.004
niacin	.014	.042

	1 tsp = 1.9 g	1 tbsp = 6.0 g
pantothenic acid	———	———
vitamin B6	———	———
folacin (mcg)	———	———
vitamin B12 (mcg)	0	0
vitamin A (IU)		

Amino Acids (grams)

tryptophan	.003	.008
threonine	.004	.013
isoleucine	.006	.019
leucine	.007	.021
lysine	.010	.030
methionine	.002	.006
cystine	.004	.012
phenylalanine	.005	.016
tyrosine	.005	.015
valine	.005	.015
arginine	.028	.087
histidine	.003	.009
alanine	.005	.014
aspartic acid	.011	.033
glutamic acid	.040	.122
glycine	.007	.022
proline	.009	.026
serine	.005	.016

OREGANO

calcium	24	71
iron	.66	1.98
magnesium	4	12
phosphorus	3	9
potassium	25	75
sodium	Trace	1
zinc	.07	.20
ascorbic acid	———	———
thiamine	.005	.015
riboflavin	———	———
niacin	.093	.280
pantothenic	———	———
vitamin B6	———	———
folacin (mcg)	———	———

	1 tsp = 1.9 g	1 tbsp = 6.0 g
vitamin B12 (mcg)	0	0
vitamin A (IU)	104	311

PAPRIKA

calcium	4	12
iron	.50	1.63
magnesium	4	13
phosphorus	7	24
potassium	49	162
sodium	1	2
zinc	.08	.28
ascorbic acid	1.49	4.91
thiamine	.014	.045
riboflavin	.037	.120
niacin	.322	1.057
pantothenic acid	———	———
vitamin B6	———	———
folacin (mcg)	———	———
vitamin B12 (mcg)	0	0
vitamin A (IU)	1,273	4,182

PARSLEY

calcium	4	19
iron	.29	1.27
magnesium	1	3
phosphorus	1	5
potassium	11	49
sodium	1	6
zinc	.01	.06
ascorbic acid	.37	1.59
thiamine	.001	.002
riboflavin	.004	.016
niacin	.024	.103
pantothenic acid	———	———
vitamin B6	.003	.013
folacin (mcg)	———	———
vitamin B12 (mcg)	0	0
vitamin A (IU)	70	303

	1 tsp = 1.9 g	1 tbsp = 6.0 g
PEPPER, BLACK		
calcium	9	28
iron	.61	1.85
magnesium	4	12
phosphorus	4	11
potassium	26	81
sodium	1	3
zinc	.03	.09
ascorbic acid	———	———
thiamine	.002	.007
riboflavin	.005	.015
niacin	.024	.073
pantothenic acid	———	———
vitamin B6	———	———
folacin (mcg)	———	———
vitamin B12 (mcg)	0	0
vitamin A (IU)	4	12
PEPPER, CAYENNE (CAPSICUM)		
calcium	3	8
iron	.14	.41
magnesium	3	8
phosphorus	5	16
potassium	36	107
sodium	1	2
zinc	.05	.13
ascorbic acid	1.38	4.05
thiamine	.006	.017
riboflavin	.017	.049
niacin	.157	.461
pantothenic acid	———	———
vitamin B6	———	———
folacin (mcg)	———	———
vitamin B12 (mcg)	0	0
vitamin A (IU)	749	2,205
PEPPER, WHITE		
calcium	6	19
iron	.34	1.02
magnesium	2	6
phosphorus	4	12

	1 tsp = 1.9 g	1 tbsp = 6.0 g
potassium	2	5
sodium	Trace	Trace
zinc	.03	.08
ascorbic acid	———	———
thiamine	.001	.002
riboflavin	.003	.009
niacin	.005	.962
pantothenic acid	———	———
vitamin B6	———	———
folacin (mcg)	———	———
vitamin B12 (mcg)	0	0
vitamin A (IU)	749	2,205

POULTRY SEASONING
(white pepper, sage, thyme, marjoram, savory, ginger, allspice and nutmeg.)

calcium	15	37
iron	.53	1.31
magnesium	3	8
phosphorus	3	6
potassium	10	25
sodium	Trace	1
zinc	.05	.12
ascorbic acid	.18	.44
thiamine	.004	.010
riboflavin	.003	.007
niacin	.045	.110
pantothenic acid	———	———
vitamin B6	———	———
folacin (mcg)	———	———
vitamin B12 (mcg)	0	0
vitamin A (IU)	39	97

PUMPKIN PIE SPICE
(cinnamon, ginger, nutmeg, allspice, clove).

calcium	12	38
iron	.34	1.10
magnesium	2	8
phosphorus	2	7

	1 tsp = 1.9 g	1 tbsp = 6.0 g
potassium	11	37
sodium	1	3
zinc	.04	.13
ascorbic acid	.40	1.31
thiamine	.002	.007
riboflavin	.002	.008
niacin	.038	.307
pantothenic acid	———	———
vitamin B6	———	———
folacin (mcg)	———	———
vitamin B12 (mcg)	0	0
vitamin A (IU)	4	15

ROSEMARY

calcium	15	42
iron	.35	.96
magnesium	3	7
phosphorus	1	2
potassium	11	32
sodium	1	2
zinc	.04	.11
ascorbic acid	.74	2.02
thiamine	.006	.017
riboflavin	———	———
niacin	.012	.033
pantothenic acid	———	———
vitamin B6	———	———
folacin (mcg)	———	———
vitamin B12 (mcg)	0	0
vitamin A (IU)	38	103

SAFFRON

calcium	1	2
iron	.08	.23
magnesium	———	———
phosphorus	2	5
potassium	12	36
sodium	1	3
zinc	———	———

Saffron contains a number of carotenoid pigments, among which are crocin and crocetin. These carotenoids manifest pro-vitamin

A activity, for they become A in the body. Saffron also has some B-complex vitamins and traces of vitamin K, copper and tin.

	1 tsp = 1.9 g	1 tbsp = 6.0 g
SAGE		
calcium	12	33
iron	.20	.56
magnesium	3	9
phosphorus	1	2
potassium	7	21
sodium	Trace	Trace
zinc	.03	.09
ascorbic acid	.23	.65
thiamine	.005	.015
riboflavin	.002	.007
niacin	.040	.114
pantothenic acid	——	——
vitamin B6	——	——
folacin (mcg)	——	——
vitamin B12 (mcg)	0	0
vitamin A (IU)	41	118
SAVORY		
calcium	30	94
iron	.53	1.67
magnesium	5	17
phosphorus	2	6
potassium	15	46
sodium	Trace	1
zinc	.06	.19
ascorbic acid	——	——
thiamine	.005	.016
riboflavin	——	——
niacin	.057	.180
pantothenic acid	——	——
vitamin B6	——	——
folacin (mcg)	——	——
vitamin B12 (mcg)	0	0
vitamin A (IU)	72	226

	1 tsp = 1.9 g	1 tbsp = 6.0 g
SESAME SEED		
calcium	4	10
iron	.21	.62
magnesium	9	28
phosphorus	21	62
potassium	11	33
sodium	1	3
zinc	.28	.82
ascorbic acid	————	————
thiamine	.019	.058
riboflavin	.002	.007
niacin	.126	.375
pantothenic acid	.018	.054
vitamin B6	.004	.012
folacin (mcg)	————	————
vitamin B12 (mcg)	0	0
vitamin A (IU)	2	5
Amino Acids (grams)		
tryptophan	.013	.038
threonine	.032	.094
isoleucine	.035	.103
leucine	.058	.172
lysine	.022	.066
methionine	.024	.072
cystine	.014	.042
phenylalanine	.041	.122
tyrosine	.030	.090
valine	.040	.118
arginine	.090	.266
histidine	.018	.054
alanine	.038	.113
aspartic acid	.061	.181
glutamic acid	.133	.395
glycine	.051	.152
proline	.037	.109
serine	.035	.105

SLIPPERY ELM
(powdered bark)   Protein 11.4 gm; fat 5.9 gm; carbohydrate
(1 cup = 80 grams)   54.6 gm;   calcium 42 mg; phosphorus 324

mg; iron 3.6 mg; sodium 2 mg; potassium 282 mg; vitamin A values unknown; thiamine .48 mg; riboflavin .11 mg; niacin .8 mg; ascorbic acid values are unknown.

SUNFLOWER SEEDS (dehulled)
(⅓ cup = 85 grams)   protein 11 gm; fat 21.7 gm; carbohydrate 9.1 gm; calcium 55 mg; phosphorus 384 mg; iron 3.3 mg; sodium 14 mg; potassium 422 mg; 20 IU vitamin A; thiamine .90 mg; riboflavin .11 mg; niacin 2.5 mg; ascorbic acids values are unknown.

	1 tsp = 1.9 g	1 tbsp = 6.0 g
TARRAGON		
calcium	18	55
iron	.52	1.55
magnesium	6	17
phosphorus	5	15
potassium	48	145
sodium	1	3
zinc	.06	.19
ascorbic acid	———	———
thiamine	.004	.012
riboflavin	.021	.064
niacin	.143	.430
pantothenic acid	———	———
vitamin B6	———	———
folacin (mcg)	———	———
vitamin B12 (mcg)	0	0
vitamin A (IU)	67	202
THYME		
calcium	26	81
iron	1.73	5 .31
magnesium	3	9
phosphorus	3	9
potassium	11	35
sodium	1	2
zinc	.09	.27
ascorbic acid	———	———
thiamine	.007	.022

	1 tsp = 1.9 g	1 tbsp = 6.0 g
riboflavin	.006	.017
niacin	.069	.212
pantothenic acid	——	——
vitamin B6	——	——
folacin (mcg)	——	——
vitamin B12 (mcg)	0	0
vitamin A (IU)	53	163

Amino Acids (grams)

tryptophan	.003	.008
threonine	.004	.011
isoleucine	.007	.020
leucine	.006	.018
lysine	.003	.009
methionine } cystine	.004	.012
phenylalanine } tyrosine	.007	.021
valine	.007	.022

TURMERIC

calcium	4	12
iron	.91	2.82
magnesium	4	13
phosphorus	6	18
potassium	56	172
sodium	1	3
zinc	.10	.30
ascorbic acid	.57	1.76
thiamine	.003	.010
riboflavin	.005	.016
niacin	.113	.350
pantothenic acid	——	——
vitamin B6	——	——
folacin (mcg)	——	——
vitamin B12 (mcg)	0	0
vitamin A (IU)		

WATERCRESS

(1 cup)　　　protein .8 gm; fat .1 gm; carbohydrate 1.1 gm;
(35 grams)　　calcium 53 mg; phosphorus 19 mg; iron. 6 mg;

(10 sprigs)   sodium 18 mg; potassium 99 mg; 1,720 IU vitamin A; thiamine .03 mg; riboflavin .06 mg; niacin .3 mg; ascorbic acid 28 mg; also traces of iodine, magnesium, manganese, sulphur, tin, aluminum and lead.

PART FOUR
Chemical Constituents

Allspice (Pimenta officinalis)
Characteristic: Resembles a blend of Cinnamon, Nutmeg and Clove; hence the name.

Constituents: A volatile oil containing about 70 percent eugenol (dental analgesic) and small quantities of eugenol methyl ether; cineol (expectorant); 1-a-phellandrene and caryophyllene; resin; tannin; fixed oil; sugar; gum; bonastre (oil); mallic and gallic acids; lignin.

Angelica (Angelica archangelica; Angelica officinalis)
Characteristic: Agreeable perfume odor (attractive to flying insects) comparable to musk or Juniper: Juniper berry flavor.

Constituents:
Root: Volatile oil (0.3–1 percent has terebangelene and other terpenes; angelic acid; valeric acid; resin (6 percent); angelicol; angelicin; xanthotoxol; starch; osthole; osthenol; archangelicin; archangin; sitosterol; and various acids: aconitic; malic; quinic; chlorogenic; caffeic; fumeric; citric; and oxalic.

Fruit: About 1 percent volatile oil; bitter substance; coumarins; resin.

Seed: Oil; methyl-ethylacetic acid; hydroxymyristic acid.

Anise (Pimpinella anisum)
Characteristic: Sweet licorice flavor and aroma.

Constituents:
Volatile (1–3 percent), consisting of about 80–90 percent anethole (anethole is light sensitive; used in soap and toothpaste; fixed oil (approx. 30 percent), consisting of traces of

methyl, chavicol and p-methoxyphenylacetone; proteins; sugars; choline; mucilage; and safrole.

Annatto (Bixa orellana)
Characteristic: Yellowish-red dyestuff with slightly pungent, acrid flavor.

Constituents:
Bixin (ethyl ester imparts rich golden-yellow color); various carotenoids that manifest vitamin A activity (similar to those found in carrots).

Basil, Sweet (Ocimum basilicum)
Characteristic: Aromatic like a mint and mildly flavored as Licorice.

Constituents:
Ocimene; other unnamed constituents similar to those in Tarragon; thymol (in Thyme). Ocimene and myricene (found in Bayberry oil) share a common empirical formula—$C_{10}H_{16}$—and are rare examples of acylic terpenes.

Bay (Laurus nobilis)
Characteristic: Forest aroma; pleasantly bitter.

Constituents:
Leaves: 1–3 percent volatile oil, which consists of cineole, pinene, eugenol, geraniol, terpenes.

Fruit: Laurel oil composed of lauryl alcohol esters of lauric, stearic, and similar acids; a volatile oil (Laurel Camphor).

Black Pepper (Piper nigrum)
White Pepper (Piper album)
Note: Black Pepper is the dried, unripe fruit of Piper nigrum. White Pepper is also derived from P. nigrum. It is the ripe fruit, partially deprived of its pericarp tissue by maceration in water, then rubbed and dried in the sun.

Characteristics:
(Black Pepper) Slightly acrid taste; somewhat pungent odor.

(White Pepper) Tastes and smells somewhat like Black Pepper only more aromatic and less pungent.

Constituents:
Black Pepper: Volatile oil; 5–9 percent piperine; piperidine; chavicine (one of the most active principles of Black Pepper); fat; proteins; resin; cellulose; starch (about 50 percent). Malic acid; tartaric acid (same as that found in grapes).

White Pepper: More starch; less ash; and oleoresin; no piperine.

Borage (Borago officinalis)
Characteristic: Has a cucumber-like fragrance and faint flavor in fresh form.

Constituents:
Small amount of oil; napthaquinones; the ureide allantoin; pyrrolizidine alkaloids; cyclitols; phenolic acids; tannins; and saline mucilage (potassium and calcium, plus other mineral acids). The fresh herb affords about 30 percent nitrate of potash and roughly 3 percent in the dried form. The saline mucilage, when cooked, leaves deposits of nitre and ordinary salt. Due to the presence of this nitrate of potash when the herb is burned, it will usually emit sparks with a slight explosive sound. For this reason it has been called "the firecracker herb."

Burdock (Arctium lappa)
Characteristic: Sweetish, mucilaginous taste to the root.

Constituents:
Inulin; (insulin substitute—root used in Soviet Union for clinical diabetes); mucilage; sugar; bitter, crystalline glucoside (lappin): resin; fixed oil; volatile oil; tannic acid; starch; lactones (sesquiterpenes); smilagenin, and sarsasapogenin; aconitic acid.

Capsicum; Cayenne Pepper (Capsicum frutescens).
Characteristic: Smells pungent and has a burning taste.

Constituents:
Capsaicin (63.2–77.2 percent); dihydrocapsaicin (21.0–32.0 percent); nordihydrocapsaicin (0.8–8.6 percent); homidihydrocapsaicin (3.2–3.6 percent); caprylic acid vanillylamide (0.1–0.6 percent); fixed oil (approx. 4–16 percent); ascorbic acid (0.1–0.5 percent); thiamine; red carotenoids (capsanthin, capsorubin);

a volatile alkaloid (capisco); oleic; palmitic and stearic acids; possibly formic acid (same factor that is found in the mandible secretions of the red ant making its bite so fiery and painful).

Caraway (Carum carvi)
Characteristic: The leaves and root are delicately flavored; seeds pungent.

Constituents:
3.5–7.0 percent volatile oil, the principal ingredient of which is carvone (50–60 percent); 20 percent fixed oil (an oxygenated oil, carvol), thymol; proteins; calcium oxalate. Carvone is also found in the oils of Dill and Cumin. Besides carvone and carvol, it has dihydrocarvone.

Cardamom (Ellettaria cardamomum)
Characteristic: Mild, pleasant, Ginger flavor.

Constituents:
Seeds: Resin; abundance of starch; 2–8 percent essential oil; 1–2 percent fixed oil.

Essential Oil: Eucalyptol (cineol); sabinene; d-a-terpineol and acetate; borneol; limonene; terpinene; l-terpinene-4-ol and its formate and acetate.

Fixed Oil: Glycerides of oleic, stearic, linoleic, palmitic, caprylic and caproic acids.

Celery Seed (Apium graveolens)
Characteristic: Aromatic odor and taste.

Constituents:
Volatile and fixed oils (2–3 percent) consisting of terpenes with smaller quantities of the anhydride of sedanonic acid, the lactone of sedanolic acid and phenols—one oil is heavy, the other lighter; apiol; the flavonoid glycoside apiin; bitter extractives; resin. Apiol is used clinically to reduce fevers.

Chili Powder (A blend)
Characteristic: Spicy and hot.

Ingredients: Chili peppers (capsicum); Cumin; Oregano (wild

Marjoram); garlic; salt, silicon dioxide (to make powder flow more freely).

Note: Consult individual spices for chemical constituents.

Chinese Angelica; Dong guei or Tang kuei (Radix Angelica sinensis)
Characteristic: The root is very oily and aromatic.

Constituents:
N-butylindenphthalide; n-valerophenone-o-carboxylic acid; n-butylphthalide-n-dodecanol; n-tetradecanol; bergapten; angelicone; angelic acid; various saponins (similar to those found in Yucca, Ginseng and Sarsaparilla); stearic acid; sucrose; myristicacae acid (found in nutmeg); and unsaturated oleic acid.

Chives (Allium schoenoprasum)
Characteristic: Delicate Onion flavor.

Constituents:
Volatile oil rich in sulphur; allicin; alliin (sulphur-containing amino acid with strong antibiotic action); trace of diosgenin which can be converted to female hormone progesterone (secreted during last half of menstrual cycle and used clinically to treat uterine hemorrhaging and to stop threatened abortion).

Cinnamon (Cinnamomum zeylanicum)
Characteristic: Warm, spicy flavor.

Constituents:
Bark: Volatile oil (0.5–1.0 percent); mannitol (sweet factor in bark); tannin; mucilage.

Oil: Cinnamic aldehyde (55–65 percent); eugenol (about 4–10 percent); terpenes; smaller quantities of other substances. As much as 80–95 percent cinnamic aldehyde could be in the oil.

Cloves (Eugenia caryophyllata; caryophyllus aromaticus; syzygium aromaticum)
Characteristic: Not spicy and penetrating.

Constituents:
Eugenol (15–18 percent); caryophyllin; gallotannic acid (10–13

percent); oleanolic acid; vanillin; eugenin; methy-n-amyl ketone (one of several minor ingredients which gives clove oil its distinctive aroma); gum; resin; fiber.

Coriander (Coriandrum sativum)
Characteristic: Pleasant lemon-orange flavor.

Constituents:
About 1 percent volatile oil; fixed oil (13 percent); calcium oxalate; tannin; malic acid; mucilage. Coriander oil contains d-linalool (60–70 percent); small amounts of geraniol and borneol; and about 20 percent of hydrocarbons, principally a- and v-terpinene.

Crab Apple (Pyrus malus; Malus communis)
Characteristic: Austere taste due to the slightly bitter, acidic juice.

Constituents:
Fruit: Starch; sugars like levulose; gallic acid; malic acid (Hydroxybutanedoic acid); amyl-valeric acid; tannins; organic salts (potash, soda, lime, etc.); traces of ammonia; qunic acid.

Seeds: Amygdaline (laetrile); mandelic acid; mandelonitrile.

Root-bark; Phloridzin (a bitter principle); quercetin (yellow-coloring matter).

Cumin (Cuminum cyminum)
Characteristic: Warm, salty-sweet; reminiscent of Caraway.

Constituents:
Volatile oil (2–4 percent); resin; gum; tannic acid; thymol; mucilage. The oil itself is limpid and pale yellow; and consists mainly of cymol (cymene) and cuminic aldehyde.

Curry Powder (A blend)
Characteristic: Pungent and spicy.

Ingredients: Coriander; Fenugreek (listed below); Turmeric; Cumin; Black Pepper; Bay; Celery seed; Nutmeg; Cloves; Onion; Red Pepper; Ginger. The ingredients can vary from country to country.

(*Note:* Consult individual spices for chemical constituents.)

Dandelion (Taraxacum officinale)
Characteristic: Leaves and flowers, acrid and bitter. Root has robust, coffee-like flavor.

Constituents:
Root: Inulin (up to 25 percent); choline; levulin; pectin; taraxacerin and taraxacin (both bitter principles); taraxerol; taraxasterol; homotaraxasterol; an enzyme capable of hydro-lyzing amygdalin (laetrile); p-hydroxyphenylacetic acid; 4-dihydroxycinnamic acid; androesterol; homoandrosterol; cluytianol; palmitic, cerotic, and melissic acids; oleic, linolic, and linolenic acids; aneurine; traces of nicotinic acid and nicotinamide; ascorbic acid (7 mg.) fresh; 0.3 mg. dried); an unnamed saponin; ceryl alcohol; lactucerol; various fatty and other acids; phlobaphenes; tannin (2.8 percent).

Flowers: Helenalin and an unidentified flavin.

Dill (Anethum graveolens; Peucedanum graveolens)
Characteristic: Aromatic and somewhat like Caraway, only milder and sweeter.

Constituents:
Volatile oil (3.5 percent), which consists of 40–60 percent d-limonene, phellandrene, carvone (a colorless liquid with a strong dill odor), and other terpenes; fixed oil protein.

Fennel (Foeniculum vulgare)
Characteristic: Pleasant Licorice flavor somewhat like Anise.

Constituents:
Volatile oil (26.5 percent); resin; gallotannic acid; stearic acid; malic acid (traces of the last two). The volatile oil contains anethole (50–60 percent), d-fenchone (appx. 20 percent), which varies in content with different species; methyl chavicol; an-ise aldehyde; anisic acid; d-a-pinene; and dipentene. Sweet Fennel oil has anethole, some limonene and phellandrene, but no fenchone; while bitter or wild Fennel oil contains hardly any anethole, but does have a little phellandrene and fenchone.

Fenugreek (Trigonella foenum graecum)
  Constituents:
  Mucilage (28 percent); bitter fixed oil (5 percent); alkaloids choline and trigonelline (metabolic breakdown of nicotinic acid but inert); lecithin, organic iron; phosphates; trimethylamine; yellow dye (unidentifiable); neurin; betaine; nucleoalbumin. Some of the chemical composition resembles that of cod-liver oil and may be used as a substitute.

Garlic (Allium sativum)
  Characteristic: Intensely strong, sulphuric odor.

  Constituents:
  Allicin: alliin (when alliin is split by the specific enzyme alliinase, an odor of Garlic develops and the fission products show antibacterial action similar to allicin); germanium (antitoxic larvicides which kill mosquito larvae); sulphur-containing compounds, some of which are found in cabbage as well. At least 33 sulphur compounds have been isolated and identified.

  Note: Allicin has incredibly strong antibacterial action equivalent to 1 percent of penicillin.
  Garlic has been used as treatment for leprosy in India and the bubonic plague in medieval Europe.

Ginger (Zingiber officinale)
  Characteristic: Aromatic; sweet-spicy; and very penetrating.

  Constituents:
  Volatile oil (1–3 percent) called gingerol (pungent, yellowish oil): shogaol (chemically related to gingerol): cineole (chief constituent of eucalyptus); citral; borneol, zingerone; traces of bisabolene, zingiberene and zingiberol (these three sesquiterpenes are principal constituents of the volatile oil); starch; acetic acid; acetate of potassa; sulphur; gum; lignin; and acrid soft resin.

Horseradish (Cochlearia armoracia; Armoracia lapathifolia; Radicula armoracia)
  Characteristic: Intensely acrid and pungent.

  Constituents:
  Contains ascorbic acid; sinigrin (which yields allyl isothio-

cyanate on hydrolysis with peroxidase or myrosinase, and enzyme from black mustard). Due to the garlic-like factor present (allyl isothiocyanate), the root inhibits the growth of microorganisms. The root also contains a bitter resin; sugar; starch; gum; albumin; and acetates.

Juniper (Juniperis communis)
Characteristic: The berries have an acrid, bitter taste. They are used in the manufacturing and distillation of gin.

Constituents:
Volatile oil (2 percent); sugar (33 percent); resin (9 percent); tannin; a flavone glycoside; juniperin; proteins; formic acid; acetic and malic acids; lignin; wax; gum; salines. The volatile oil contains alcohols (50 percent), chiefly 1-terpinen-4-ol, plus a-pinene, camphene, and cadinene.

Kelp (Fucus versiculosus)
Characteristic: Slightly saline and sea-weed tasting.

Constituents:
Carrageenan (found in Irish moss also); galactitol; galactose; uronic acid; sulphuric acid; agarose; and agaropectin; starch; fat; protein; alginic acid; and kainic acid.

Lemon Balm (Melissa officinalis)
Characteristic: When the fresh herb is bruised, it gives forth a strong lemon fragrance.

Constituents:
Volatile oil consisting of aldehyde and citronellal. The oil in this plant emits considerable ozone, which makes it an excellent surgical dressing. The chemical hydrocarbons contain so little oxygen that in wounds dressed with Lemon Balm oil the germ microbes are virtually asphyxiated. Furthermore, the plant resins of Lemon Balm dry upon contact with a wound, neatly sealing it.

Lovage (Legusticum scoticum)
Characteristic: Strong odor and warm, aromatic flavor similar to Celery.

Constituents:
Volatile oil; angelic acid (found in angelica); ligulin (coloring principle); resins; and coumarin derivatives (coumestrol).

Mace (Myristica fragrans; Arillus myristicae; Myristicia officinalis; Myristica moschata).
Characteristic: Strong Nutmeg flavor and smell.

Constituents:
Aromatic balsam (24.5 percent); volatile oil (4–15 percent) essentially identical to that of nutmeg oil; macilenic acid; macililic acid; protein; gum; resins; glucosides (sugars); safrole.

Marjoram, Wild or Oregano (Origanum vulgare)
Marjoram, Sweet or Marjoram (Origanum marjorana; Marjorana hortensis)
Characteristics:
(Oregano): Acrid and pungent; strong sage-like aroma reminiscent of Thyme.

(Marjoram): Faint Sage-like odor; slightly Minty aftertaste.

Constituents:
Oregano: Thymol; borneol; linalool; pinene; cineol; thujone.

Marjoram: Volatile oil; menthol; thymol; di- and tri-terpenoids; saponinas; puridine and pyrrolidine alkaloids; carvacrol; insect-molting hormones; polyphenols; tannins; iridoids; quinones; furanoids; cyclitols; coumarin; sugars (raffinose and stachyose). All in small amounts.

Mustard White (Brassica alba; Brassica hirta; Sinapis alba)
Mustard, Black (Brassica nigra; Sinapis nigra;)
Characteristics:
White Mustard: Mildly pungent.

Black Mustard: Strongly pungent.

Constituents:
White Mustard: Volatile oil which is yellowish to begin with, but acquires a brighter yellow when mixed with alkali; a glucoside, sinalbin; syrosin; moisture causes decomposition to occur and brings about the formation of new chemicals (acrinyl), isothiocyanate, sinapine hydrogen sulphate and glu-

cose); fixed oil (30 percent), consisting of the glycerides of oleic, stearic, and brassic (eruic) acids; proteins (25 percent); mucilage. The glucose, sinalbin, and the enzyme, myrosin, unite to form a volatile oil themselves. When this oil is cold, it has a faint, Anise-like aroma, but acquires a definite pungency when heated.

Black Mustard: Acrid, volatile oil which contains sulphur, some myrosin and sinigrin; volatile oil in seeds is about 0.7–1.3 percent and also contains over 90 percent of allyl isothiocyanate (garlic compound); fixed oil (27 percent); traces of sinapine hydrogen sulphate; brassic (erucic), behenic, and sinapolic acids; proteins (30 percent); mucilage.

Nutmeg (Myristica fragrans; Myristica officinalis)
Characteristics: Sweet spiciness and pleasant taste.

Constituents:
Fixed oil (25–40 percent); starch; proteins; lignin; stearin; gum; volatile oil (5–15 percent) consists of the following: syristicin, elemicin, eugenol, isoeugenol, methyleugenol, methylisoeugenol, and methoxyeugenol. Nutmeg also contains safrole and myristic acid.

Onion (Allium cepa)
Characteristic: Distinctive odor due to the sulphur-containing volatile oil.

Constituents:
Quercetin (yields phloroglucin and protocatechuic acid upon decomposition with air; quercertin-mono-d-glucoside and quercetin-3-glucoside; tannin; saponin; hydrocyanic acid; cyclo-alliin; propanethial S-oxide (forms sulphuric acid when dissolved with water; this explains the onion's tearful aspect, when this particular chemical comes in contact with the water in the eyes); pyruvic acid (this tear-inducing factor is only formed when Onion tissue is cut, chopped, minced, etc.); prostaglandin A; rubber content of 0.14 percent.

Onion Seeds: allylpropyl bisulfide; S-(1-propanyl) cysteine sulfoxide; 1-propenylsulfenic acid.

Paprika, Hungarian (Capsicum annuum)
Characteristic: Sometimes tasteless, sometimes pungent and slightly sweet.

Constituents:
Capsaicin (69 percent); dihydrocapsaicin (22 percent); nordihydrocapsaicin (7 percent); homo-capsaicin (1 percent); capsanthin. Paprika contains more ascorbic acid (vitamin C) than regular Capsicum does. The plant also contains solanine and chlorogenic acid.

Parsley (Petroselinum sativum)
Characteristic: Sweet, mildly spicy and refreshing.

Constituents:
Root: Starch; sugar; mucilage; volatile oil; apiin.

Seeds: Volatile oil (more than in the root—2.6 percent); fixed oil; apiol (dimethoxysafrole); apiolin; apiin; tannin.

Leaves and herb: Ethanol; hex-3-en-l-yl acetate; cis-3-hexen-l-ol.

Peppermint (Mentha piperita)
Characteristic: Entire plant has a distinct aroma due to the volatile oil. A hot, aromatic sensation is at first experienced; but it may be distinguished from spearmint by the coolness which is felt immediately afterwards in the mouth.

Constituents:
Volatile oil (1–1.5 percent); tannin; resin; gum. The oil consists of 50–78 percent free menthol and from 5–29 percent combined in various esters (menthone found in older plant tissues, slowly disappears and menthol accumulates, replaced by menthyl acetate); menthyl acetate principal ester which gives the oil its agreeable Minty aroma); acetaldehyde; isovaleraldehyde; ascetic acid; valeric acid; a-pinene; phellandrene; cineol; l-limonen; d-and l-menthone; menthly isovalerate; cadinene; amyl alcohol; and dimethyl sulfide.

Pickling Spice (A blend)
Characteristic: Pungent and spicy.

Ingredients: Cinnamon; Allspice; Mustard; Coriander; Bay

leaves; Ginger; Chilies; Cloves; Black Pepper; Mace; Carda mom.

Note: Consult individual spices for constituents.

Pumpkin spice (A blend)
Characteristic: Warm and agreeable; pleasantly sweet and mildly spicy.

Ingredients: Cinnamon; Ginger; Nutmeg; Allspice.

Note: Consult individual spices for constituents.

Rosemary (Rosmarinus officinalis)
Characteristic: Refreshing; piny; resinous; pungent.

Constituents:
Approximately 1 percent volatile oil (borneol and linalool, 10–18 percent); bornyl acetate, etc.; 2–5 percent cineole (eucalyptal) about 20 percent; pinene; camphene; resin; bitter principles.

Saffron (Crocus sativus)
Characteristic: Exhibits an exotic, but delicate, pleasantly bittersweet flavor.

Constituents:
About 1 percent volatile oil (the oil in the stigmas and petals contains at least 34 known components, which include various terpenes, terpene alcohols, and esters); a bitter sugar compound, picrocrocin; a red-coloring matter, crocin (polychroit), which has pro-vitamin A activity; fixed oil; wax; glucose; gentiobiose and crocetin.

Sage, Common Garden (Salvia officinalis)
Characteristic: Pungent; warm; astringent.

Constituents:
1–2.5 percent volatile oil (terpene, thujone, camphor, salvene, pinene, cineol); terpene predominates in the fresh oil, but thujone and camphor predominate if the oil is left standing; resin; tannin; bitter principle .

Savory, Summer (satureia hortensis)
Savory, Winter (Satureia montana)
    Characteristics:
    Summer Savory: Warm; aromatic; resinous; delicate Sage flavor.

    Winter Savory: Stronger than Summer Savory in all of the above.

    Constituents:
    (Both): About 20 percent thymol; 30–40 percent carvacrol; menthol; di- and tri-terpenoids; saponins; a few pyridine and pyrrolidine alkaloids; insect-molting hormones; polyphenols and tannins; iridoids; quinones; furanoids; cyclitols; coumarin; and the sugars raffinose and stachyose.

Sesame (Sesamum indicum)
    Characteristic: Toasted; nutlike flavor.

    Constituents:
    50 percent fixed oil (oleic acid, linoleic acid, palmitic and stearic acids); sesamin; sesamolin.

Slippery Elm (Ulmus fulva)
    Characteristic: The inside bark smells like Fenugreek and has a somewhat bitter taste, and peculiar odor like Lovage or wild Celery. It has an extremely mucilaginous, dull flavor.

    Constituents:
    Considerable mucilage composed of D-galactose (1 part), 3-0-methyl-D-galactose (19 percent), L-rhamose (2 parts), and D-galacturonic acid (2 parts); starch; tannins; calcium oxalate; and calcium.

Spearmint (Mentha spicata)
    Characteristic: Slightly pungent and aromatic; but lacking the cool sensation experienced when chewing fresh mint leaves.

    Constituents:
    Volatile oil (approx. 0.5 percent) contains between 50–55 percent carvone, -limonene, phellandrene, dihydro-carveol acetate, and various esters of acetic, butyric, and caprylic acids; resin; tannin.

Sunflower Seeds (Helianthus annuus)
Characteristic: Nut-like, slightly oily and somewhat sweet taste.

Constituents:
Semi-drying, oleic-linoleic acid oil (50–60 percent) consisting of: palmitic acid (6.4 percent); stearic acid (1.3 percent); arachidic acid (4.0 percent); behenic acid (0.8 percent); oleic acid (21.3 percent); linoleic acid (66.2 percent). The glycerides in Sunflower oil consist mainly of mixed triglycerides, each containing 1 or 2 linoleic acid radicals; linolenic acid (0.1 percent); mixed tocopherols (vitamin E) about 75 milligrams to 100 grams of Sunflower oil (this comes close to the tocopherol content of wheat germ oil, which is 103 mg/100 grams). Sunflower seeds also contain small amounts of inulin; large quantities of levulin; and other plant sugar compounds; plus tannin.

Tarragon (Artemisia dracunculus)
Characteristic: Licorice-Anise flavor; pleasant, slightly bitter.

Constituents:
B-Allylanisole (estragole; methyl chavicol); ocimene, myrcene; phellandrene; p-methoxycinnamaldehyde. The herb yields up to 0.8 percent oil of Tarragon.

Thyme (Thymus vulgaris)
Characteristic: Strong; pleasant, pungent Clove flavor.

Constituents:
Volatile oil (1–2.6 percent); resin; tannin; gums. Thymol is the main factor which gives the herb thyme its distinctive flavor. Carvacrol is also found in oil of Thyme. It too has a thymol odor.

Turmeric (Curcuma longa)
Characteristic: Aromatic; pepper-like; acrid; mildly warm; woody-spicy aroma.

Constituents:
Curcumin (yellow coloring matter); p, p-dihydroxydicinnamethane; p-hydroxycinnamolyferuloymethane; dicaffeoylmethane; caffeoylferuloylmethane; p,a-dimethylbenzyl alcohol; l-methyl-4-acetyl-l-cyclohexene; turmerone; a-phellandrene;

sabinene; zingiberene cineol; borneol; caprylic acid; sugar compounds—arabinose fructose (12 percent), and glucose (28 percent).

Watercress (Nasturtium officinale)
Characteristic: Yields a pleasing, peppery taste.

Constituents:
Volatile oil rich in sulphur and nitrogen; Garlic-like allyl compound (sulphur-cyanide); saponin; tannin; erucic acid (represents up to 80 percent of the fatty acids present in watercress); some unidentified compounds found in the *Brassica* family (cabbage species).

Appendix

How to Collect, Dry
and Prepare Herbs and Spices

The Complete Book of Spices so far has provided medical, nutritional and culinary informatin about herbs and spices. The first part of the following appendix describes methods of preparing plants for medicinal use as ointments, tinctures, fluid extracts, infusions or teas, decoctions or powders. These instructions are printed with the kind permission of Max G. Barlow, and taken out of his book *The Shepherd's Purse*, © 1979, McGammon, Idaho. They are followed by brief recommendations for preparing herbs and spices for use in the kitchen.

COLLECTION

The active medicinal principle or virtue of a plant varies with such physical and environmental factors as:

Light
Temperature
Season and Seasonal Fluctuations
Elevation
Moisture, etc.

The time of day must be considered for the same reason. Plant chemicals change as the basic plant physiology changes from morning to night. Most plants can be collected in the morning after the dew and other moisture has evaporated.

The plant should be dried as soon after collecting as possible to prevent mildew or fermentation, which alters the plant's medicinal properties.

Only healthy looking plant parts should be used. Brown, unhealthy or discolored plant parts should not be collected.

Collections should be made away from busy, populated areas. This will help insure your collected plants will be free from sprays, toxins, and other harmful substances which may have been absorbed into the plant tissues.

Most plant parts above the ground (bark, seeds, stems, leaves and fruits) need not be cleaned. Underground parts should be thoroughly washed to prevent dirt from becoming part of the plant preparation.

After the plant is completely dried it should be stored away from air, moisture, warm temperatures and light, all of which are factors that promote plant deterioration. Most dried plants are hydroscopic (absorb moisture from the air) and therefore need to be stored in airtight containers.

When possible, the entire plant should be used as each part imparts an essential virtue to the total medicinal action. This is especially meaningful with annual plants.

Roots should be collected in the early spring before the vegetative growth process has begun, or in the fall when all vegetative growth has ceased.

When a dried plant is cool to the touch, it is not completely dry.

Drying temperatures and time of drying should be adjusted to the individual plant. Coarse plants may take considerably longer than fragile, tender plants. 89°F. to 102°F., 32° to 39°C. is called "gentle heat" and is considered optimum.

Leaves
Collect when the flower is beginning to open.

Temperatures

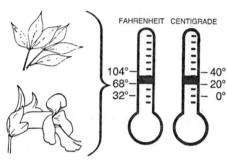

Flowers
Collect just before flower is fully expanded.

Stems (herbaceous)
Collect when the flower is beginning to open.

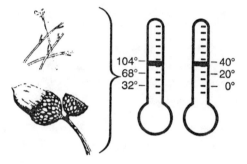

Seeds and Fruit
Collect when fully ripe.

Bark
Collect in early spring or in the fall when all vegetative growth has ceased.

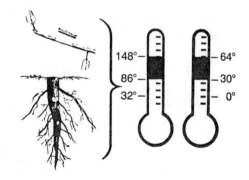

Roots
Collect in early spring or in the fall when all vegetative growth has ceased.

OINTMENT PREPARATION

Definition: Ointments are semi-solid preparations for external application. They are derived from animal or vegetable oils and also from petroleum bases with other supplemental substances added to make them more usable.

Modern bases are available which make excellent ointment preparations. Various noncommercial ointment substances can be obtained in your own locality without much difficulty.

Ointment Bases:

1. Lanolin (wool fat)
2. Goose grease
3. Lard
4. Olive oil
5. Sesame seed oil
6. Cotton seed oil
7. Hydrogenated vegetable oil
8. Peanut oil
9. Safflower oil
10. Mineral oil
11. Petrolatum (petroleum jelly)
12. Glycerin

To give the above ointment bases firmness beeswax (white or yellow) and paraffin wax are supplemental additives. The amount of these hardeners added depends upon how climatically hot it is during the summer.

Equipment needed to compound usable ointment.

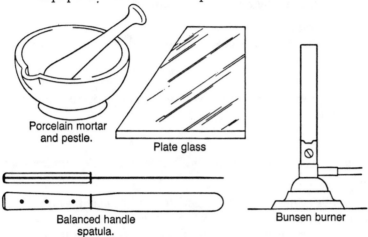

Porcelain mortar
and pestle.

Plate glass

Balanced handle
spatula.

Bunsen burner

**Methods of getting medicinal plant substances into the
ointment base.**

METHOD I. PREPARATION BY INCORPORATION

STEP 1.
Reduce the medicaments into a fine powder (see pages 157–158.)

STEP 2.
Select ointment base for your particular purpose.

STEP 3.
Use a small portion of base to be used. Gradually incorporate
the powder to form a smooth nucleus. Continue to add base to
obtain right texture and consistency.

METHOD II. PREPARATION BY FUSION.

STEP 1.
Prepare a water bath (using a double boiler-type pan) to melt
the fusion ingredients. For example, beeswax, paraffin, lanolin.
Start melting the materials with the greatest fusion temperatures and add those materials with lower melting points.

STEP 2.
Remove from heat (a safe distance away from heat source) and
slowly add fine, powdered herb.

STEP 3.
Stir constantly while adding medicament.

STEP 4. (Optional)
If necessary, strain to remove unwanted material. Use clean, fine-woven cloth.

STEP 5.
Stir until preparation is homogenous and cooled to a uniform, thick ointment.

Depending upon your application, the following classifications are made:

Non-penetrating ointment—used for epidermal therapy. It is needed especially where a protective emollient is indicated.
Example: petrolatum, waxes or a combination of both.

Deep-penetrating ointment—used to penetrate into the deep layers of the skin. They are indicated when inflammation is present.
Example: vegetable oils, lard, lanolin or combination of these.

TINCTURE PREPARATION

Definition: Tinctures are preserved plant extracts produced by soaking a given amount of plant material (usually in powdered form) in direct proportion to an extracting solution (usually alcohol) called the menstruum. It is sometimes referred to as a dilute fluid extract.

Standard Tincture (Procedure A or B)

Ratio of plant material to menstruum. 1 gram to 10 ml.

1.5 ounces to 1 pint (English)   } Workable
45 grams to 500 milliliters (metric) } quantities

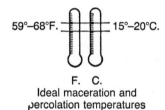

59°–68°F.   15°–20°C.

F.   C.
Ideal maceration and
percolation temperatures

PROCEDURE A

Maceration Technique:

STEP 1.
Macerate indicated amount plant material with proper amount of menstruum. Make sure bottle or container has a good sealing top.

1 pt. of
alcohol
(500 ml.)

147

STEP 2.
Let material soak for approximately 2 weeks at temperatures listed as ideal, above. Keep away from the direct sunlight.

STEP 3.
Shake bottle twice each day.

STEP 4.
Decant and filter extract. Pour off supernatant into a clean bottle. Where possible, express liquid from plant into bottle.

STEP 5.
Cork (or rubber stopper), label and store safely. Be sure to seal container tightly with an adequate sealing lid. Store in a safe place away from small children.

Menstruum

1½ oz. of plant material

Extracted plant material.

Tincture (finished product)

Label:
Tincture of_____
Date of Preparation_____
Preparation Method_____
Not for Sale—for private use by producer only.

PROCEDURE B

Percolation Technique:

STEP 1.
Place desired amount of plant material (powdered or green) into a mixing jar.

STEP 2.
Add enough menstruum to uniformly moisten material.

STEP 3.
Macerate for twenty-four hours.

STEP 4.
Place moist plant material in a conical percolator. Pack firmly to where percolation is not slow or too rapid.

STEP 5.
Check rate of percolation. (see page 151).

1.5 ounces of plant material in soaking menstruum

STEP 6.
Add sufficient menstruum to percolate
500 milliliters (1 pint) in receiving jar.

STEP 7.
Cap bottle and label for storage and
future use (see step 5, Procedure A).

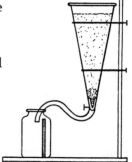

NOTE: Tinctures and fluid extracts calling for alcohol preparations should use only ethyl alcohol or grain alcohol. **Denatured
or wood alcohols must not be used for they are toxic and
poisonous.** Care must also be taken not to have an open flame
near alcohol for it is very flammable and can cause serious burns
to the skin.

FLUID EXTRACT

Definition: An alcohol preparation of a vegetable extract containing the active constituents in a definite ratio of plant material to solvent. It is sometimes called a 100% tincture.

Standard Fluid Extract

Ratio of plant material to menstruum—1 gram to 1 milliliter of menstruum.

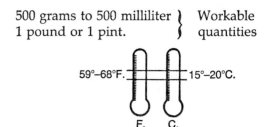

500 grams to 500 milliliter ⎫ Workable
1 pound or 1 pint. ⎭ quantities

59°–68°F. — 15°–20°C.

F. C.

PROCEDURE A

STEP 1.
Macerate powdered or granulated plant material in appropriate menstruum.

STEP 2.
Soak for 10 days (or as specified). Keep away from direct sunlight and keep temperature at ideal range.

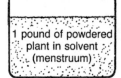

1 pound of powdered plant in solvent (menstruum)

Cover to
prevent
evaporation

STEP 3.
Express (squeeze) through a clean cloth into a container. Filter into a bottle and cap or cork to seal. Label.

PROCEDURE B

Follow steps 1 and 2 of Procedure A.

STEP 3.
Using a conical percolator, first place a filter paper in the lower "neck" of the apparatus. Sometimes a sterile rock or pebble is placed next to hold the filter paper in place. (Depending on the nature of the percolate, a menstruum soaked piece of cotton can be placed in the neck of the percolator.)

STEP 4
Pack moist plant material into the perculator. Pack firmly to where rate of perculation is at desired speed. If the amount of moistened plant material will adequately fit in the percolator, maceration can be done within the percolator.

STEP 5.
When percolation is to begin, add sufficient menstruum to percolate through the plant mass until the extracted fluid reaches the predetermined height in the calibrated receiving bottle. Two or three percolations can be accomplished with the original plant material before it is totally exhausted. (Each extraction is of course less potent than the previous one.)

STEP 6.
Cap bottle and label.

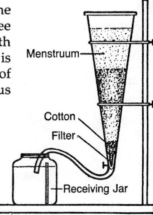

Conical percolation

Menstruum

Cotton

Filter

Receiving Jar

INFUSION PREPARATION

Definition: Infusions are aqueous solutions of plant extracts prepared at a temperature just below the boiling point. The plant material may be dried or moist. Like decoctions, infusions are temporary extracts, and unused portions should be discarded after several hours. An infusion is commonly called a "tea."

Standard Infusion
> 50 grams (coarsely comminuted) plant material in 1000 cc of distilled water.
> Workable ratio: 1½ ounces of plant to 1 quart of water.

PROCEDURE A

STEP 1.
Place ground plant into a suitable glass or stainless steel container.

STEP 2.
Pour in just enough cold water to moisten plant material.

STEP 3.
Bring distilled water to a boil and pour over moistened plant material.

STEP 4.
Let steep for 15 minutes, then pass product through a strainer.

PROCEDURE B

STEP 1.
Place 1½ ounces of leaves, flowers, and/or stems into a suitable container. Add 1 quart of cold water.

STEP 2.
Add heat. When water begins to boil, remove from heat and let cool for 5 minutes or until it cools to drinkable temperature.

STEP 3.
Strain and express juices through a strainer into a quart jar.

STEP 4.
Add enough water to fill quart capacity.

Cup   Tea Kettle

DECOCTION PREPARATION

Definition: Decoctions are aqueous solutions of plant extracts prepared at a boiling temperature. They differ from infusions generally in that roots and other coarse plant structures make up the decoction substances. This is a temporary extract and should not be kept more than 5 to 6 hours. Make a fresh preparation as needed.

Standard Decoction

> 50 grams (generally of coarsely comminuted) plant material in 1000 cc of cold water.
> Workable ratio: 1½ ounces of plant to 1 quart of water.

PROCEDURE

STEP 1.
Place ground plant into a suitable vessel provided with a cover (lid). Never use aluminum or iron cookware. Porcelain or heat-resistant glassware is preferred.

STEP 2.
Pour in one quart (1000 cc) of cold water. Mix to uniformity.

STEP 3.
Place container over heat. Once material comes to a boil, set timer for 15 minutes of boiling time.

STEP 4.
Remove from heat and cool to about 100°F.

STEP 5.
Pour decoction through a strainer, expressing juices from the plant material. You should have slightly less than the 1000 cc,

so pour additional cold water over the "marc" through the strainer and into the holding vessel until the 1 quart level is reached.

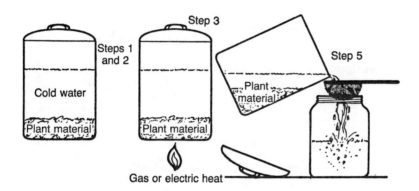

POWDER PREPARATION

Definition: Plants reduced in size to meet requirement for inclusion into capsules, ointments, and infusions, etc., is called powdering.

General Powdering Information

Select only good quality plant materials. They should be free from dirt, dust, and other adulterants. Brown or diseased plant parts should not be used.

Powdering should be done just prior to the user's actual need for the plant's medicinal values. The active principle dissipates with the passage of time to about 12 to 15 percent per year. No powder should be kept over four years.

Plant material should be extremely dry before the powdering process begins. Powdering is best accomplished with reduced environmental temperatures (in an air-conditioned area or during colder seasons).

Weight for weight, powdered plant is more potent than a herbaceous green plant. This is because the green plant has a high water content. To determine the ratio of green plant potency to dry plant strength, weigh the green plant before and after dessication. The weight difference will indicate the potency differences. For example, if one half of the weight is lost to drying, figure the green plant was 50 percent less potent than the same amount of the dried and powdered plant material.

A problem with storing powdered botanicals is they must be stored so moisture and insects will not cause them harm. This problem can be solved by placing the dried plant in a clean paper bag and putting this bag in a sealable, plastic bag.

Remember that fine powdered plants can be very flammable and should be kept away from open fire, or gas burners.

When trying to reduce gummy or resinous plants to a powder, it may be necessary to add a little ether or high proof alcohol to the plant which allows it to be broken down into smaller particles without the sticky problems.

Practice will greatly enhance your skill in using powdered plants. Since your work is for your own private use and not for sale or marketing, use only small amounts of the plant, reserving your collected plant for future use.

Powdering Methods:

(A) PRE-REDUCTION PREPARATION OF PLANTS.

Some plant parts should be reduced in size while they are still green and freshly collected. Slicing and cutting to expose more surface area for drying can also serve to reduce the size of the plant for milling or grinding.

Mills and plant grinders are available which are designed to reduce plant to granules or to fine powders. Some are hand powered while others are electrically powered.

In many cases a hammer or mallet can
reduce the dried plant to a size suitable for pulverizing by other powdering methods. Dried roots, coarse bark
and thick stems can be comminuted by
this technique.

(B) FINE REDUCTION TECHNIQUES.

After the plants have been reduced to a
fairly small granular mass, or a more or
less semi-coarse powder, a mortar and
pestle can be used to further reduce the
particle size.

A spatula can be used to reduce particle size while incorporating medicaments
into ointments and salves.

PREPARATION FOR DRAWING SALVE

INGREDIENTS:

Beeswax—the size of a walnut
Pine (conifer) resin—1 part (qt.)
Mutton tallow—1 part (qt.)

GENERAL USES:

For blood poisoning
For infection (sores) both man and animal
For hemorrhoids (external use)

PROCEDURE:

1. Obtain fresh mutton tallow (not beef tallow).

2. Render out the tallow (melt into an oil condition).

3. Strain through a loose weaved cloth (an old clean dish towel will do).

4. Strain into a clean one gallon container for use or for future use. Will store indefinitely without going rancid.

5. When ready to use: Re-melt in a cast iron pan (skillet). After mutton is melted, turn temperature to low heat or simmer.

6. Add equal part of pine resin.

CAUTION: DO NOT BOIL (Keep temperature on low or simmer once mutton has melted.)

7. Stir until oil and resin are completely blended.

8. Shave in beeswax (about ¾ of block).

9. Mix in well by stirring.

10. Strain again (to remove resin impurities) and pour into a clean gallon container which will serve as a pouring container.

11. Pour into smaller jars. Pour before salve becomes cool.

12. Leave to cool and solidify overnight. When solidified, it is ready to use.

Obtaining Basic Ingredients

Mutton tallow: May be obtained from those who raise sheep or a slaughter house.

Pine gum or resin: May be obtained from any pine, spruce, or fir tree as follows:

In late May or early June, pine sap flows.

With a sharp instrument, notch a V-shaped cut into the tree and place a can or other collecting receptacle to catch the bleeding or running resin. Select an older tree for cutting. Pinus monophylla produces excellent gum resins which can be picked from the tree or from the ground.

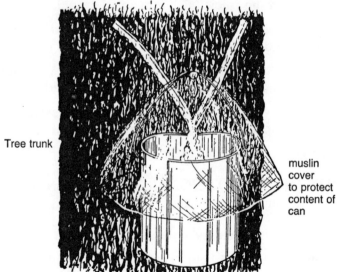

Tree trunk

muslin cover to protect content of can

Drying and Freezing Herbs and Spices

Leaves to be dried and used in the kitchen should be picked on a sunny morning just after the dew has dried—never in the rain. They can be dried in several ways: hung upside down in bunches near the ceiling in a warm room away from the sun; the leaves can be spread out in trays and put in a 100°F. oven with the door slightly open; or they can be spread out in trays and left in a warm dark room until dried. Wherever they are dried, air must circulate about them. They are ready to be stored when they crackle when rubbed between fingers. Trays must be labeled separately, as dried leaves resemble each other very closely.

Seeds are treated slightly differently: branches are hung in clusters with paper bags tied around the bottom or seed section of each cluster. As the clusters dry, the seeds drop from the plant into the bag. When they are all collected, they are put in a strainer to shake out any dirt or scraps of flower or leaf. Then the seeds dry out on trays in an airy non-sunny place for a couple of weeks. Both seeds and leaves should always be kept separate from each other and labeled carefully in airtight jars.

It is also possible to pack leaves tightly in airtight containers or small plastic bags and freeze, nicking off a piece as needed. They must be thoroughly dry before freezing. The flavor lasts longer if the plants are freshly picked.

Bibliography

BOOKS

A Barefoot Doctor's Manual. 1977. Philadelphia: Running Press.

Adams, Catherine F. November 1975. *Nutritive Value of American Foods in Common Units: USDA Agricultural Handbook no. 456.* Washington: U.S. Government Printing Office.

Airola, Paavo. 1976. *How to Get Well.* Phoenix, AZ.: Health Plus Publishers.

Angier, Bradford. 1978. *Field Guide to Medicinal Wild Plants.* Harrisburg, PA.: Stackpole Books.

Brendle, Thomas R. and Unger, Claude W. 1935. *Folk Medicine of the Pennsylvania German: The Non-Occult Cures.* Norristown, PA.

Chopra, R. N., *et al.* 1958. *Chopra's Indigenous Drugs of India.* Calcutta: U. N. Dhur & Sons Private, Ltd.

Christopher, John R. 1976. *School of Natural Healing.* Provo, Utah: Christopher Publications.

Claus, Edward P., Tyler, Varro E. and Brady, Lynn R. 1970. *Pharmacognosy.* Philadelphia: Lea & Febiger.

Clowes, William. 1591. *A Proued Practice for All Young Chirungiens.* London.

Culbreth, David M. R. 1927. *A Manual of Materia Medica and Pharmacology.* Philadelphia: Lea and Febiger.

Curtin, L. S. M. 1965. *Healing Herbs of the Upper Rio Grande.* Los Angeles: Southwest Museum.

D'Andreto, Carlo. 1968. *Herbs and Other Medicinal Plants.* Italy.

Descourtilz, M. E. 1833. *Flore Pittoresque et Medical des Antilles.* Paris. (8 volumes.)

Editing Committee on Chinese New Drugs. 1978. *Chinese New Drugs.* Hong Kong.

Elliott, Douglas B. 1976. *Roots—An Underground Botany & Forager's Guide.* Old Greenwich, CT: Chatham Press.

Erichsen-Brown, Charlotte. 1979. *Use of Plants for the Past 500 Years.* Aurora, Ontario (Canada): Breezy Creek Press.

Flück, Hans. 1976. *Medicinal Plants.* London: W. Foulsham & Co. Ltd.

163

Freeman, Margaret B. 1943. *Herbs for the Mediaeval Household for Cooking, Healing and Divers Uses.* New York.

Gerard, John. 1975. *The Herball or Generall Historie of Plantes.* New York: Dover Publications. (First published London, 1633.)

Gibbons, Euell. 1973. *Stalking the Faraway Places.* New York: David McKay Co.

Gibbons, Euell. 1974. *Stalking the Good Life.* New York: David McKay Co.

Gibbons, Euell. 1973. *Stalking the Healthful Herbs.* New York: David McKay Co.

Grieve, Maude. 1971. *A Modern Herbal.* New York: Dover Publications. (2 volumes)

Grime, William Ed. 1976. *Botany of the Black Americans.* St. Clairs Shores, MI: Scholarly Press, Inc.

Gunn, John C. 1901. *Gunn's New Family Physician.* Philadelphia.

Harris, Ben Charles. 1971. *Better Health with Culinary Herbs.* New York: Weathervane Books and Barre, MA: Barre Publishing Co.

Heinerman, John. 1977. *Medical Doctors' Guide to Herbs.* Orem, UT: Bi-World Publishers.

Heinerman, John. 1980. *Science of Herbal Medicine.* Orem, UT: Bi-World Publishers.

Heinerman, John. 1980. *Treatment of Cancer with Herbs.* Orem, UT: Bi-World Publishers.

Hermann, Matthias. 1973. *Herbs and Medicinal Flowers.* New York: Galahad Books.

Hewitt, James. 1972. *Everything You Want to Know about Sea Foods.* New York: Pyramid Books.

Hoffer, A. and Osmond, H. 1967. *The Hallucinogens.* New York: Academic Press.

Hutchens, Alma R. 1973. *Indian Herbology of North America.* Windsor, Ontario, Canada: Merco.

Hylton, William H. 1978. *The Rodale Herb Book.* Emmaus, PA: Rodale Press.

Indoor Gardening at the Hippocrates Health Institute. Boston: Hippocrate Health Institute.

Industrial Microbiology. 1976. New York.

Jain, S.K. 1968. *Medicinal Plants.* New Delhi, India: National Book Trust.

Kaslof, Leslie J. 1978. *Wholistic Dimensions in Healings.* New York: Doubleday/Dolphin.

Kjaer, K. 1976. *The Biology and Chemistry of the Cruciferae.*

Kloss, Jethro. 1975. *Back to Eden.* Santa Barbara, CA: Woodbridge Press.

Krochmal, Arnold and Connie. 1973. *A Guide to the Medicinal Plants of the United States*. New York: Quadrangle/ The New York Times Book Co.

Law, Donald. 1970. *Herbs for Cooking and Healing*. North Hollywood, CA: Wilshire Book Co.

Law, Donald, 1975. *Herbs for Health and Flavor*. New York: St. Martin's Press.

Lehane, Brendan. 1977. *The Power of Plants*. Switzerland.

Levey, M. 1955. *Chemistry and Chemical Technology of Ancient Mesopotamia*. Amsterdam.

Lewis, Walter H. and Elvin-Lewis, Memory P. F. 1977. *Medical Botany*. New York: John Wiley & Sons.

Lloyd, Francis E. 1976. *The Carnivorous Plants*. New York: Dover Publications.

Lundwall, Nels Benjamin. 1974. *Faith Like the Ancients*. Salt Lake City, UT: Mountain Valley Publishers.

Majno, Guido. 1975. *The Healing Hand—Man and Wound in the Ancient World*. Cambridge, MA: Harvard University Press.

Marsh, A.C. *et al.* 1977. *Composition of Foods: Spices and Herbs—Raw, Processed, Prepared*; USDA Agricultural Handbook No. 8–2. Washington, D.C.: U.S. Government Printing Office.

Merck Index. 1976. Rahway, NJ: Merck & Co.

Mitton, F. and V. 1976. *Mitton's Practical Modern Herbal*. London.

Moyer, Joanne, 1973. *Nuts and Seeds: The Natural Snacks*. Emmaus, PA: Rodale Press.

Neithammer, Carolyn. 1974. *American Indian Food and Lore*. New York: Collier Books.

Porcher, Francis Peyre. 1863. *Resources of the Southern Fields and Forests—A Medical Botany of the Confederate States*. Charleston, SC: Evans & Cogswell.

Proceedings of the 10th National Conference on Wheat Utilization Research. November 1977. Tucson, AZ.

Quelch, Mary Thorne. 1969. *Herbs for Daily Use*. London: Faber & Faber, Ltd.

Reppert, Bertha P. 1976. *A Heritage of Herbs*. Harrisburg, PA: Stackpole Books.

Rogers, S. 1975. *How to Grow and Use Herbs*. Toronto: Coles Publishing Co., Ltd.

Rosengarten, F., Jr. 1973. *The Book of Spices*. Wynnewood, PA: New York: Pyramid Books.

Sherman, John A. 1979. *The Complete Botanical Prescriber*. Corvallis, OR: Corvallis Naturopathic Clinic.

Singer, C. *et al.* 1965. *A History of Technology*. Oxford.

Sloane, H. 1707–25. *The Natural History of Jamaica*. London. (2 volumes)

Spoerke, David G. 1980. *Herbal Medications*. Santa Barbara, CA: Woodbridge Press.

Soepardi, R. 1957. *Obat-obatan dari hasil Hutan (Medicines from Forest Products*. Djakarta, Indonesia: Government Publishing House.

Teteny, P. 1970. *Infraspecific Chemical Taxa of Medicinal Plants*. New York.

Thomson, William A.R. 1978. *Medicines from the Earth—A Guide to Healing Plants*. Switzerland.

Trease, George E. and Evans, William Charles. 1978. *Pharmacognosy*. London: Bailliere Tindall.

Vallery-Radot, R. 1900. *La vie de Pasteur*. Paris.

Wagner, H. and Hörhammer, L. 1971. *Pharmacognosy and Phytochemistry*. Berlin: Springer-Verlag.

Wagner, H. and Wolff, P. 1977. *New Natural Products and Plant Drugs with Pharmacological, Biological or Therapeutical Activity*. Berlin: Springer-Verlag.

Wallis, T.E. 1967. *Textbook of Pharmacognosy*. London: J & A. Churchill, Ltd.

Watt, John Mitchell and Gerdina-Breyer-Brandwijk, Maria. 1962. *The Medicinal and Poisonous Plants of Southern and Eastern Africa*. Edinburgh: E. & S. Livingstone, Ltd.

Wentzel, George L., Sr. 1966. *Wentzel's Menu Maker*. Austin, TX: George L. Wentzel Publishing.

Wheelright, Edith Grey. 1974. *Medicinal Plants and Their History*. New York: Dover Publications.

Williamson, Darcy. 1978. *How to Prepare Common Wild Foods*. McCall, ID: Darcy Williamson Publisher.

Wilson, Charles O., Gisvold, Ole and Doerge, Robert F. *Textbook of Organic Medicinal and Pharmaceutical Chemistry*. Philadelphia.

Wiseman, Richard. 1686. *Several Chirurgical Treatises*. London.

Wren, R.W. 1972. *Potter's New Cyclopaedia of Medicinal Herbs and Preparations*. New York: Harper Colophon Books.

JOURNALS AND PERIODICALS

Allen, Mary B. and Dawson, E. Yale. 1960. Production of anti-bacterial substances by benthic tropical marine algae. *Journal of Bacteriology* 79:459.

American Review of Soviet Medicine I:236–50. February 1944.

Amygdalin (laetrile). 1973. *Science* 182;1000

Andrene, Meinrat O. 1978. Distribution and speciation of arsenic in natural waters and some marine algae. *Deep-Sea Research* 25:391–401.

The battle of the beers. *Time*. September 4, 1978. pp. 60–71.

Black pepper kills bugs. *Agricultural Research*. May 1978. p. 15.

Blaine, George. January 1947. Experimental observations on absorbable alginate products in surgery. *Annals of Surgery* 125:102; 113–4.

Brendle, Thomas R. and Unger, Claude W. 1935. Folk medicine of the Pennsylvania German; the non-occult cures. *Proceedings of the Pennsylvania German Society* 45:392,91, Pt. II. Morristown, PA.

The Canadian Pharmaceutical Journal. October 1888.

(Capsicum) *Chemical Abstracts* 91:313, entry #3567. July 30, 1979.

Chandler, L.J. *et. al.* 1979. Herbal remedies of the Maritime Indians. *Journal of Ethnopharmacology* 1:49–68.

Chang, Stephen. April 1980. *Sciquest*, p. 17.

Connor, William E. *et al.* July 1978. The plasma lipids, lipoproteins, and the diet of the Tarahumara Indians of Mexico. *The American Journal of Clinical Nutrition* 31:1131–1142.

Cooney, Robert V. *et al.* September 1978. Arsoniumphospholipid in algae. *Proceedings of the National Academy of Science* 75:4262–64.

Cosmetics and Toiletries 95:79.

(Dandelion Flowers) *Archives of General Psychiatry* 16:1; 10, 24, 1967.

(Dandelion Flowers) *Proceedings of the Third World Congress of Psychiatry* 1:619, Montreal 1961.

Foster, R. F. The need for biological monitoring of radioactive waste streams. *Sewage Industrial Wastes* 31:1409–15.

Frantz, Virginia K. June 1948. Experimental studies of alginates as hemostatics. *Annals of Surgery* 127:1165–72.

Gerdawskene, L. L. *et al.* Consumption of freeze-dried foods in weightlessness. *Kosmicheskaya Biologiya I Aviakosmicheskaya Meditsina* (Space Biology and Aerospace Medicine) no. 2, Moscow 1978; pp. 25–28.

Goldway, William J. March 1981. Bleeding gums. *Bestways*. p. 18.

Govindarajan, V. S. Turmeric chemistry, technology, and quality. C.R.C. *Critical Review in Food Science and Nutrition* 12:277; 291–95.

Harney, John W. *et al.* July-August 1978. Behavioral and toxicological studies of cyclopentanoid monoterprenes from Nepeta Cataria. *Lloydia* 41:373.

Hennekens, Charles H. *et al.* Effect of beer, wine and liquor in coronary deaths, and Castelli, W. P., How many drinks a day?, both in *Journal of the American Medical Association* 242:1973–74; 2000, November 2, 1979.

Highton, T. C. 1963. The effect of seragrom patients with rheumatoid arthritis on carrageenan granuloma pouches, skin wounds and weight gain in rats. *British Journal of Experimental Pathology* 44:137.

Holmes, E. M. October 1884. Medicinal plants used by the Cree Indians at Hudson's Bay. *The Pharmaceutical Journal and Transactions*. pp. 302–4.

Houck, J. C. *et al.* August 1960. The inhibition of pepsin and peptic ulcers. *Gastroenterology* 39:196.

Into onion: tears and therapies. *Science News* 115:265, April 21, 1979.

Jackson, Basil and Reid, Alan. February 17, 1969. Catnip and the alteration of consciousness. *Journal of the American Medical Association* 207:1349–50.

Jain, R.C. and Konar, D.B. February 1978. Effect of garlic oil in experimental cholesterol atherosclerosis. *Atherosclerosis* 29:125–29.

Jain, R.C. July 1975. Garlic in alloxan-induced diabetic rabbits. *The American Journal of Clinical Nutrition* 28:684.

Jaros, S. J. and Dwey, J. L. April 1964. Uses of an alginate in hyposensitization. *Annals of Allergy* 22:173–74; 178–79.

Journal of the American Medical Association 146:760, June 23, 1951.

Kennedy, John G. Tesquino complex: the role of beer in Tarahumara culture. *American Anthropologist* 65:620–623.

Kruse, Olene. May-June 1979. Kickabrew grow juice. *The Mother Earth News* no. 57.

Lawrence, Brian M. *Essential Oils 1976–1978.* Illinois, 1979. p. 7.

Lorenz, Klaus. December 1980. Cereal sprouts; composition nutritive value, food applications. *Critical Reviews in Food Science and Nutrition* 13:353–385.

(Lovage) *Critical Reviews of Food Science and Nutrition* 13:246. 1980.

(Lovage) *Science* 126:970. November 8, 1957.

Marsh, A. C. *et al.* 1977. Composition of foods: spices and herbs— raw, processed, prepared. *USDA Agricultural Handbook* no. 8–2. Washington, D.C.: U.S. Government Printing Office.

Murphy, Elizabeth W. *et al.* February 1978. Nutrient content of spices and herbs. *Journal of the American Dietetic Association* 72:174–176.

Myakado, Masakazer *et al.* 1980. Insecticidal joint action of pipercide and co-occurring compounds isolated from pipernigrum L. *Agricultural and Biological Chemistry* 44:1703.

The New Physician, November 1980.

Nicolarchuk, L. V. and Kosuik, E. S. 1980. Phytodieletics and phytotherapy in diabetes and their future use. *Therapeuticheski Arkhiv* 52:110–11.

Nielsen, Steeman, 1955. *Marine Biology and Oceanography Deep Sea Research* 3:281.

Oliver, Leslie C. January 1950. Haemostasis with absorbable alginates in neurosurgical practice. *British Journal of Surgery* 37:307.

(Onion Seeds) *Indian Journal of Nutrition and Dietectics* Volume 12, 1975.

Passe and Blaine, October 23, 1948. Alginates in endaural wound dressing. *Lancet.* p. 651.

Plato, Phillip and Denovan, James T 1974 The influence of potassium on the removal of 137 Cs by live chlorella from low level radioactive wastes. *Radiation Botany* 14:37.

Robertson, Wm. Van B. and Schwartz, Barry. 1953. Ascorbic acid and the formation of collagen. *Journal of Biological Chemistry* 201:689–96.

Ryther, John H. Fuels from marine biomass. *Oceanus—The International Magazine of Marine Science.* 22:49–58, 79/80.

Schiff, E. and Herschberger, C. 1938. *Journal of the American Medical Association* 110:244.

Shih, Ling and Harris, Natholyn D. Antimicrobial activity of selected antioxidants. *Cosmetics and Toiletries* 95:75–79.

Sigerist, Henry E. February 1944. Ambroise Pare's onion treatment of burns. *Bulletin of the History of Medicine* 15:143–49.

Smith, Clifton A.H. May 17, 1946. A new and effective hemostatic agent. *Science* 103:634.

Solandt, O. M. 1947. Some observations upon sodium algivate. *Quarterly Journal of Experimental Physiology* 31:26; 28–29.

Swift Meat Company. 1951. *Chemical Abstracts* 45:7723–24.

Thienes, Clinton H. *et al.* 1957. The hemostatic laxative and toxic effects of alginic acid preparations. *Archives Internationales de Pharmacodynomie et de Therapie* 111:167–181.

(Turmeric) February, 1980. *Cosmetics and Toiletries* 95:79.

Wei-cheng, Hsu. May 1977. Garlic slice in repairing eardrum perforation. *Chinese Medicinal Journal* 3:204–5.

Weihrough, John L. and Gardner, John M. July 1978. Sterol content of foods of plant origins. *Journal of the American Dietectic Association* 73:40.

Williams, George. 1957. A histological study of the connective tissue reaction to carrageenan. *Journal of Pathology and Bacteriology* 73:557–63.

Wisswaesser, Catherine. April 1977. Roots and ramifications of medicinal herbs in 18th century North America. *Transactions of Studies of the College of Physicians of Philadelphia* 44:194–95.

Wood, Larry. May-June 1977. Farming giant kelp. *Sea Frontiers* 23:159–66.

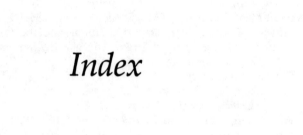

Index

Index

Abdominal cramps (*See also* Indigestion; Intestinal gas), 1: basil, 19; cumin, 32; dill, 33; fennel, 34; ginger, 38; juniper, 41; marjoram, 47–48; pickling spice, 52, 53; spearmint, 60; white pepper, 66

Abortion, 1: black pepper in induction, 20; chives in prevention, 29

Abscess,1: slippery elm, 59

Acne, (*See* Blood purifiers; Rash)

Addiction (*See* Alcoholism; Drug addiction)

Adjuvants for herbs, 1: 27, 34

Adjuvants for laxatives (*See* Aperients)

Alcoholic beverages (*See also* Beer; Wine), 78–81: antiseptic value, 78–79; blood cholesterol and, 79–80

Alcoholism (*See also* Cirrhosis of liver), 1: angelica, 15; Chinese angelica, 28; thyme, 63

Alfalfa, sprouting, 88, 89

Allergies (*See also specific condition, e.g.*, Hives), 1: burdock, 22; slippery elm, 58

Allspice: characteristics, 14, 123; constituents, 123; medical applications, 1, 2, 4, 6, 7, 9, 10, 12, 13, 14–15; mineral/vitamin content, 98; non-medical applications, 15; parts used, 14

American saffron, 54

Amino acids: basil, 99–100; dill, 105; fennel seed, 106–7; fenugreek seed, 107–8; garlic powder, 108; ginger, 109; grain sprouting and, 86; mustard seed, 111–12; onion powder, 113; sesame seed, 119; thyme, 121

Anemia, 1: angelica, 15; chives, 29; dandelion, 32; fenugreek, kelp, 42; watercress, 65

Angelica (*See also* Chinese angelica): characteristics, 15, 123; constituents, 123; medical applications, 1, 2, 3, 4, 5, 6, 7, 8, 9, 10, 11, 12, 13, 15–17; non-medical uses, 17; parts used, 15

Anise: as bait, 18; characteristics, 17, 123; constituents, 123–124; medical applications, 2, 3, 4, 5, 6, 7, 8, 9, 12, 13, 17–18; mineral content, 99; non-medical uses, 18; parts used, 17

Annatto: characteristics, 18, 124; constituents, 124; medical applications, 7, 8, 9, 11, 13, 18; parts used, 18

Antibacterial/antibiotic agents (*See also* Infection[s]), 1: garlic, 36, 130; kelp, 42; sage, 54

Antidote for strong herbs, 1: coriander, 30

Antioxidant(s): allspice, 15; in food preservation, 83; rosemary 15, 83; sage, 15, 83

Antiseptic(s), 1: alcoholic beverages as, 78–79; basil, 19; garlic, 36; juniper, 40; onion, 49; white mustard, 48

Aperients, 1: allspice, 14; black pepper, 21; coriander, 30; pumpkin pie spice, 53

Appendicitis, 1: fenugreek, 35; slippery elm, 58

Appetite stimulation, 1: allspice, 14; angelica, 15; anise, 17; capsicum, 23, 24; caraway, 26; celery seed, 27; coriander, 31; dandelion 32; dill, 33; fennel, 34; garlic, 38; horseradish, 39; juniper, 40; marjoram, 47; rosemary, 53; saffron, 54; tarragon, 62; white mustard, 48

Arsenic in wine, 81

171